THE PORCH AND THE CROSS

Kevin Vost

THE PORCH
AND THE CROSS

*Ancient Stoic Wisdom
for Modern Christian Living*

✝

Foreword by
Kenneth J. Howell

Preface by
Jared Zimmerer

 Angelico Press

Cover image: James Tissot (French, 1836–1902)
Gentiles Ask to See Jesus, Brooklyn Museum,
Purchased by public subscription, 00.159.202
Cover design: Michael Schrauzer

CONTENTS

Acknowledgments

I would like to thank Sister Matthew Marie Cummings, O.P., and Sister Elizabeth Anne Allen, O.P., for introducing me to Angelico Press when I was provided the opportunity to review and endorse their edited volume, *Behold the Heritage: Foundations of Education in the Dominican Tradition* (Angelico Press, 2012). Many thanks to Angelico's publisher, John Riess, for saying yes to this book idea on a topic perhaps a bit unusual for a modern Catholic publisher. Thanks as well to my editor, Sam Wigatow, and to all the Angelico staff who helped bring this book to print.

Thanks are due as well to Dr. Kenneth Howell and Jared Zimmerer for the thoughtful foreword and preface they provided. Thanks as always to my friend and sometimes co-author Shane Kapler, who labored on his complementary tome, *The Epistle to the Hebrews and the Seven Core Beliefs of Catholics* (Angelico, 2016), and provided support, advice, and encouragement while I plugged away on this one.

I would also like to express gratitude to Patrick Ussher, a Ph.D. student at the University of Exeter in England with a great knowledge and passion for the practical wisdom of the Stoics, the editor of the book *Stoicism Today: Selected Writings* (CreateSpace, 2014), and manager of the Stoicism Today website blog, for posting on their site a chapter I had written on the Stoics from a previous book on my reversion story, and for allowing me to mention that this book was forthcoming.

Last and never least, I'd like to thank my wife Kathy for all that she did and endured like a Stoic over those many months in which my nose was stuck inside old books while my fingers clicked noisily away at the keyboard. (I think old Epictetus himself would have been proud of her.)

Foreword

THERE IS A WIDESPREAD NOTION today that science and/or philosophy are in conflict with religion, specifically the Christian religion, a notion that is rarely questioned in the popular media. When I taught classes on science and religion in two public universities over the years, I regularly encountered students who had bought into this notion. Why? Part of the answer is historical. The idea that there is a conflict between science and religion began in earnest in the Enlightenment of the 18th century but it became an unquestioned fact by the opening decades of the 20th century. Even so brilliant a thinker as Bertrand Russell naively bought into the warfare narrative. So, it is not surprising that such would be the common belief among students.

If we look at science, or more broadly human reason, from a wider historical perspective, we discover some astounding facts. Prior to the 17th century, there were very few hints of any potential conflict between human reason and the Christian faith. In fact, in the Middle Ages, faith and reason were seen as complementary ways of arriving at truth. Though this belief was at times tested, most medieval thinkers embraced the idea of compatibility. This did not mean, however, that faith and reason were believed to be the same thing, or to teach the same truths. These thinkers made clear distinctions. What it did mean was that the Christian mind did not reject truths of reason because they were not specifically religious.

* Angelico Press wishes to thank Dr. Howell for contributing Forewords to both *The Porch and the Cross* and Shane Kapler's complementary volume, *The Epistle to the Hebrews and the Seven Core Beliefs of Catholics*. Taken together, these works seek to show how Providence made use of philosophy to ready the Gentile, and divine revelation the Jew, to receive and live the fullness of the truth revealed in Christ. The modern Christian requires both solid philosophical reasoning and unmitigated faith in God's word to undertake the New Evangelization and return the western world to its Foundation; may these two works be means toward that end.

The Porch and the Cross

The attitude in the Middle Ages had in fact been adopted centuries earlier by Christian thinkers who were steeped in the philosophical traditions of the ancient Greeks. From Justin Martyr in the second century to Augustine in the fifth and beyond, the early Christian thinkers embraced all that was true and good in pagan philosophy. One of the most fruitful examples of this rapprochement occurred in the case of Stoic philosophy.

Kevin Vost has chosen to focus on the ancient Stoic philosophers. He makes it abundantly clear that the Stoics drew on and developed their own natural reason to such a degree that they discovered many moral truths without the aid of the Christian religion. The choice to focus on the ancient Stoics is not an arbitrary one, for the Stoics were philosophers as the ancients conceived philosophy to be. Modern academic philosophy has become dry and sterile in many of its compartments. The ancients in general conceived of philosophy as a way of life, as a reflective guide to living well (*bene vivendi*). This included the study of nature, or what we call science today, as well as logic and ethics.

The Stoics have much wisdom to teach us moderns. This fact can be seen in the revival and application of Stoic wisdom in certain circles of modern psychotherapy. Like the modern therapist, the Stoics concentrated on the question of what it meant to live well. One foundational belief of the Stoics was the idea that for human beings to live well they must live in accord with their own nature and the nature of the world around them. This can be seen in one of Vost's protagonists, the emperor-philosopher Marcus Aurelius:

> He who does not know what the cosmos is does not know where he is. He who does not know from what the cosmos has sprung does not know who he is nor what the cosmos is. He who lacks one of these does not know where he has sprung from. Who then seems to be the one who flees or pursues the praise of those who make noise, who know neither where they are nor who they are. (*Meditations*, book 7, no. 52)

The idea that human happiness was tied to the nature of things in the universe was a common assumption of most of ancient philosophy, but it has been largely rejected or neglected in the modern world. Since the time of David Hume and Immanuel Kant, most people think of morals as subjective opinions that have nothing to do with nature. One doesn't have to cite examples of how people today imagine that what they think in their heads is more real or true than the objective truths around them in the wider world and imprinted in their own bodies.

Careful engagement with the Stoics can show us that human reason needs to be guided by objective facts and realities. And this is what those early Christian thinkers realized. It is also what allowed them to adopt and adapt those natural truths of reason in the service of their Christian faith. It is not too much of an exaggeration to say that this act of putting human reason at the service of faith was what gave birth to the universities in the Middle Ages. The University of Paris in the 12th century, for example, grew out of three monasteries where ancient Greek learning was combined with Christian theology. The truths of natural reason and the truths revealed by God in the Christian faith are not the same truths, but they are compatible with one another.

Joseph Ratzinger (Pope Benedict XVI) was a leading intellect in Germany when he lived and taught there many years ago. Being a man who understood this history, he saw clearly how relevant it is for the world today. Once he said, "The appeal to reason is a great task for the Church, especially today, for whenever faith and reason part company, both become diseased." This book is an attempt to heal the rift between natural reason and Christian faith by taking the reader back to the Stoic thinkers as a complement to natural law and Christian faith.

KENNETH J. HOWELL

Preface

CULTURES AND CIVILIZATIONS across the ages and globe can often find agreement on one of the most important factors of being a living, human being, something that is so dear to our very core that the delineating dissimilarities fall flat at the feet of this one congruent aspect of daily living: relationship. The Hebrews held their relationship to the one, true God as the epitome of human purpose and fulfillment. The ancient Greeks and Romans held relationship as the foundational principle of sound reasoning and dialogue in order to perfect their ideals of virtue. And indeed, I must gleam the profound importance of a friendship such as mine with the likes of Kevin Vost and Shane Kapler. Through the common bond of constant search for truth and finding it in the heart of Christ incarnate, I have been able to form a companionship with these two men that has led to sound communal reasoning and recognition of the Divine reality within God's revealed word. Their dynamic duo of literary works—Shane's *Hebrews and the Seven Core Beliefs of Catholics*, and Dr. Vost's *The Porch and the Cross*—focus on the prominence of faith and reason, which St. John Paul II called the "two wings of a dove." It brings to mind the image of an ancient Stoic sitting at the foot of Mount Olympus, having a reasoned and revelatory discussion with one of the ancient Hebrew prophets, as he looks to the skies above Mount Zion!

Kevin Vost has become a leading voice in promulgating the wisdom of the great Doctor of the Church, St. Thomas Aquinas. Thomas had a deep love of the Greek and Roman philosophers. It is in the spirit of Thomas's great mind that Kevin dives into the lives and lessons of a few of the prodigious Stoics. With the Church, Kevin

---

* This preface also appears in Shane Kapler's *The Epistle to the Hebrews and the Seven Core Beliefs of Catholics.*

resoundingly affirms that truth is truth, no matter who says it. And indeed, the Stoics Kevin discusses knew a great deal of rational, God-given truth; so it is of utmost importance that we continue their legacy of consistently searching for that which will fill our lives with purpose. Kevin, in his uniquely personable writing style, does an incredible job bringing to life the instructions of men who lived nearly 2,000 years ago! It is as if they were writing for our time and our culture, a vivid demonstration of truth's timeless nature.

Personally, I have read quite a bit of the Stoics, but I must admit that I have never had their lessons presented in such a relatable and subjective way. With Kevin revealing a bit about these men's lives, and then relating their message to the indomitable Catholic faith, I found myself coming to revere these men on a much deeper level. I gained even more respect for what they were able to accomplish with natural human reason. I think the most important message, the one that simply oozes from *The Porch and The Cross*, is that the ideals of proper living, loving, and thinking in which these Stoics were so well-versed ought to be a guiding light in a time such as ours. The time in which these teachers lived is more similar to our time than what one might think: morals were washed over with relativism; expressions of love were seen as commerce; and the desire for comfort trumped the necessity of virtue. And yet these men stood tall and strong against such a wave of weakness, preaching the truth that they were able to identify as a gift from God. From Kevin's relating of each of these Stoic lessons to the message of the Cross of Christ—and the Church established by Christ's sacrifice— we see that ultimate wisdom and knowledge of human nature and proper living are ultimately fulfilled in searching for and modeling our own lives off of the discipleship of Jesus, which guarantees our own crosses. It seems that the Stoics would be right next to the likes of St. Thomas Aquinas, cheering us on to pick up our crosses and embrace the struggle of right living in accordance with reason to become the virtuous images of God we were created to be. Which then brings me to the next book in our forceful duet, Shane Kapler's *Hebrews and the Seven Core Beliefs of Catholics*.

While I may be commenting on Shane's book second in this foreword, it is in accordance with the practice of presenting ideas in their order of importance. As St. John Paul II so fittingly explained, "The lesson of history in this millennium now drawing to a close shows that this is the path to follow: it is necessary not to abandon the passion for ultimate truth, the eagerness to search for it or the audacity to forge new paths in the search. It is faith which stirs reason to move beyond all isolation and willingly to run risks so that it may attain whatever is beautiful, good and true. *Faith thus becomes the convinced and convincing advocate of reason.*"[1] It is faith that ultimately fulfills what philosophy cannot. It is similar to running a race: when nearing the end, there is nothing left in your physical tank, and it takes something beyond natural inclination to push ahead and finish strong. This is where the faith presented in the Letter to the Hebrews can instruct the accomplished and even mountainous wisdom of the Stoics. Faith is more than just the icing on the cake, it is the yeast which makes it rise!

Shane's unbelievable depth of knowledge regarding Catholicism's first-century Jewish roots was first unveiled in his book *Through, With, and In Him: The Prayer Life of Jesus and How to Make It Our Own*. This new work, expounding upon the seven core beliefs of Catholics as the fulfillment of God's revelation to the Jewish people, concretizes my respect for Shane's work, and my adoration for God's plan overflows! As Catholic Christians we desire to fulfill our Lord's command of "One Faith, One Lord, One Baptism" (Eph. 4:5). A thorough knowledge of our Hebrew ancestors allows us to find common ground with our Protestant brothers and sisters in Sacred Scripture. By unveiling Catholicism's core beliefs within the pages of Scripture—most particularly the reality of Christ's True Presence in the Holy Eucharist and the authority of our ordained leaders—Shane gives us the tools to have a deeper, more significant discussion about the true Church of Jesus Christ. This book offers more than just a profounder understanding of our Jewish roots; it proposes a mental removal of the veil of the Holy of Holies—completing the Jewish understanding of salvation with the exposed and tangible new sanctuary of Christ's body and bringing Jewish faith and the practice thereof to its definitive fulfillment.

1. *Fides et Ratio* (italics added).

7

By continuously linking the rituals and beliefs of the Hebrew people to the written word of God in the Book of Hebrews, Shane boldly indicates the undeniable bond between the Chosen People and the New Covenant in Christ Jesus. The Letter to the Hebrews is a powerful work, surrounded by mystery and containing such striking verses as 4:12: "Indeed, the word of God is living and effective, sharper than any two-edged sword, penetrating even between soul and spirit, joints and marrow, and able to discern reflections and thoughts of the heart." In a truly Catholic spirit, this book builds upon the great prophets of old; in reading it you will find yourself immersed in a world that integrates the best of the ancient with the core of faith in Christ.

I am proud to say that I have been a co-author with these two gentlemen of reason and faith, but I am even more honored to say that I call them friends. When we came together to write *Man Up! Becoming the New Catholic Renaissance Man*, I knew that these two men were gifted and magnetic in their writing and their characters. I can't recommend these two new books enough. I challenge you to do your best to see how God works in the history of mankind through and with the great minds of the past, as well as through his own revelation to his chosen ones. As Christians, as human beings, we must do our part in searching out the heights and the depths of truth. We can do so with the gift of natural human reason so long as it is wrapped in and elevated by the grace of faith. In this way, we can discover the horizon that St. John Paul II desired all of us to reach: "Only within this horizon of truth will people understand their freedom in its fullness and their call to know and love God as the supreme realization of their true self."[2]

JARED ZIMMERER

---

2. *Fides et Ratio*, 107.

Author's Preface
Greeks Seeking Wisdom
(and Finding It in Rome)

Because it was in Greece that the most sublime wisdom flourished, as it is said in the Epistle to the Corinthians: "The Jews require signs, and the Greeks seek after wisdom."

~ St. Albert the Great[1]

For it is not the hearers of the law who are righteous before God, but the doers of the law who will be justified. When Gentiles who have not the law do by nature what the law requires, they are a law to themselves, even though they have not the law. They show that what the law requires is written on their hearts. . . .

~ St. Paul, Letter to the Romans 2:13–15

Greeks Seeking Wisdom under the Porch

THE OLD TESTAMENT of the Bible tells the story of God's special relationship with his "chosen people," the Jews, and how he provided them with special signs, instructions, and miraculous interventions that would guide them toward truth and toward moral behaviors that would prepare them for the coming of Truth Himself in the incarnation of "the Word," of "the truth, and the way, and the life," in the person of the Messiah and Savior, Jesus Christ.[2]

---

1. Cited in Joachim Sighart, *Albert the Great: His Life and Scholastic Labours: From Original Documents,* (Charleston, SC: Bibliolife, 2009), 302 (referencing 1 Cor. 1:22).

2. I direct you to my friend Shane Kapler's companion volume, *Hebrews and the Seven Core Beliefs of Catholics* (Angelico Press, 2016), for a fascinating examination of this revelational Hebrew heritage as evidenced in the New Testament Letter to the Hebrews.

The Bible tells us as well that God was the Creator and Father of all men and women, and not only of the Jews. *Only* humans and *all* humans are made in the image and likeness of God,[3] in that we are graced in our natures with intellect and will—with means to discern the true and to choose to act upon the good. In those same centuries before the birth of Christ during which God was preparing his chosen people for the coming of His Son, other people throughout the world used their intellects and wills, guided by God-given natural reason, to discern the true and act on the good without benefit of such direct revelation. Those who pursued truth most diligently and penetrated most deeply into its heart were, as St. Albert tells us, the Greeks.

The so-called "pre-Socratic" Greek philosophers of the 7th–5th centuries BC, such as Thales, Anaximander, Pythagoras, Heraclitus, Parmenides, Anaxagoras, and others, were largely "natural philosophers" or "physicists," essentially pioneering scientists who sought to explain through reason the nature of the universe. With Socrates (c. 470–399 BC) came a special focus on philosophy as a literal *philos* (love) of the kind of *sophia* (practical wisdom) that sought how human beings could live good, joyful, and virtuous lives. Socrates' most prominent student, Plato (429–347 BC), and Plato's student prodigy, Aristotle (384–322 BC), also examined the good life, but like the pre-Socratics they studied many other things as well, such as natural philosophy or science, metaphysics (the issues that go beyond physics, like why there are laws of physics in the first place), issues of logic and of epistemology (the theory of knowledge, or how we know what we know), and more.

Ten years before the death of Aristotle, a child named Zeno (332–262 BC) was born in the city of Citium, on the island of Cyprus in the far eastern Mediterranean Sea. Around the year 300 BC he set up his philosophical shop on the north side of Athens' marketplace under the *Stoa Poikile,* the world-renowned "Painted Porch" decorated on its inner walls with paintings and sculptures of epic Greek battles by the famous artists Micon of Athens and Polygnotos of Thasos. From within the colonnade of this amazing porch he taught

3. Gen. 1:26–27.

three main branches of philosophy—logic, physics, and ethics—but for Zeno, and for his "Zenonian" followers who would later become known as the "Stoics" because of the place of their philosophy's birth on the stoa, the greatest of these was *ethics*.

Logic and physics were essentially handmaidens to ethics; not to academic, hair-splitting, ivory-tower, theoretical ethics, but to the kind of practical ethics that help us live lives of moral virtue in accordance with nature. "Happiness is a good flow of life," said Zeno, and this flow is attained by properly using our human reason (*logos*) in accord with the Logos with a capital "L"—we might say, the Logos of Universal Reason, that some Stoics would come to call "God."

Zeno was influenced primarily by the lives and lessons of two earlier Greeks: Socrates himself, and the founding father of the Cynics, Diogenes of Sinope (412–323 BC), via Zeno's Cynic teacher, Crates of Thebes (365–285 BC). Diogenes and his followers were called Cynics—from the Greek *kynikos*, meaning "dog"—because of the simple, natural, nearly animalistic lives that some of them led. They embraced poverty and simplicity in very extreme ways. It was Diogenes who slept in Athens' marketplace in a big ceramic jar. It was he who, when Alexander the Great had sought him out, asked the conqueror to step aside so he'd stop blocking his sun! More moderate than the Cynics, Zeno and later generations of his Stoics blended Cynic and Socratic ideals in the sunny islands of Greece; yet the bulk of the lives and lessons within this book derive not from Greece, but from Rome.

The Porch and the Cross Come to Rome

"All roads lead to Rome," as the medieval saying goes, and we find this to be as true in the history of Stoicism as it is in the history of Christianity. The cross spread to Rome in the first century after Christ's birth via his two greatest apostles, St. Peter and St. Paul. The porch moved there as well and at around the same time, via the four great Stoic expositors we'll examine in the pages ahead. Many readers may be familiar with some of St. Peter and St. Paul's exploits in Rome; their building up of the Catholic Church; one's letter to

Romans; the other's letter from Rome; and at their lives' ends, their martyrdoms there as well. Probably less familiar to Christian readers, though common knowledge to any modern friends of the Stoics who may chance upon these pages, is the fact that all four of the major Stoics we'll meet also lived a large part of their lives in Rome; and indeed, one was, in a sense, martyred there too.

Those who know the Stoics only by name and through second- or third-hand sources at that may know them as dead ancient men, non-emotional, Spock-like sourpusses who tried to keep a stiff upper lip as they plodded through isolated lives without affection and joy. As we'll see in the chapters ahead, this could hardly be farther from the truth. Their powerful life lessons live on. They call out across all boundaries of place and of time if we but take the effort to hear them. They have wisdom to share with each and every one of us. They can teach us to live calmer, happier, more productive, humane, noble, and virtuous lives whether we live in Rome, Italy, in Athens, Greece or in Athens, Illinois.[4]

4. Just a couple miles from my home in Springfield. (Population 1,726 according to the 2000 census.)

On the Nature of This Book

With everything which entertains you, is useful, or of which you are fond, remember to say to yourself, "What is its nature?"

~Epictetus, *Encheiridion*[1]

IF ALL GOES AS PLANNED, you will find this book entertaining and useful, and grow fond of it, partly because it relays the fascinating wit and wisdom of Epictetus himself, along with three other noble philosophers, one his teacher, another his student across time. They have helped me immensely in the most practical and profound of professional and personal ways. The teachings of these ancient preacher-teachers of the public forum changed me from the most nervous, heart-pounding, trembling-voiced lecturer into a relaxed public speaker, happy to talk to an audience of any size without a single written note. These doctors of the soul helped me conquer natural tendencies toward worry and sadness. These seekers of truth, beauty, and goodness helped rescue me from twenty-five years in a bland atheistic wilderness as their musings from under the porch helped opened my eyes once again to the ultimate truth, beauty, and goodness of the cross of Christ.

In the pages ahead I'll flesh out these personal stories just a bit, share more stories of other modern souls moved by these ancient seekers of wisdom, and show how their wisdom may help enhance your life as well; but first let's take a look at our modern world and ask ourselves a few probing questions.

---

1. Chapter 3, in *Epictetus: Discourses Books III–IV, The Encheiridion*, trans. W. A. Oldfather (Cambridge, MA: Harvard University Press, 2000), 487. (First published in 1928. Volume One includes introductory material and Books I–II of the *Encheiridion*. Further references to the set will specify Oldfather v. 1. or v. 2.)

The Porch and the Cross

Is Your Smart Phone
Smart, As Smart As a Stoic?

We in the West are the blessed and fortunate inheritors of profoundly intertwined Judeo-Christian and Greco-Roman traditions that recognized and honored the inherent powers of intellect and will within the human soul. These dual pillars of civilization have fostered startling and exciting achievements in the worlds of science and technology, developing at such a pace that much of the technology we take for granted today exceeds the wildest fancies of futuristic thinkers but a few decades ago. (Just watch some old sci-fi movie from the 1950s and you'll see how lame, limited, clunky, and old-fashioned their spaceships' controls and computers look compared to the phone in your pocket.) We've certainly come a long, long way since the days of the dusty ancient Hebrews and Greeks seeking the signs and the wisdom of their day—*but are we more peaceful, joyful, caring, happy human beings?* (And isn't that what really matters?)

Ironically, a potential pitfall of our modern technology, of having a world of electronic information at our fingertips, is that we may feel no need to learn about the thoughts and ideas that made such a world possible. Further, taking the modern ways of the world for granted, those who feel unhappy and unfulfilled may have little clue that there *is* timeless wisdom to be mined in the thoughts of the ancients. So many of us today have but the slightest knowledge of the great minds and grand ideas that laid the foundations for what is good about the modern world, and which also hold the answers to many of the ills that still plague the human soul. We need to ask ourselves if our "smart phones" are smart enough to answer questions like these, or if even the vast and seemingly all-knowing Internet itself could supply us the right answers if we were to put questions like these into the search bar:[2]

---

2. I actually put several of these questions into the search bar, and the results were not impressive. When I entered "Why is there so much distress, anxiety, violence, and unhappiness in the world?" potential answers on the first page included articles on "the culture of affluence," "irritable male syndrome," and "concussive brain trauma." When I entered "Is there a God?" the first page of entries alone included the answers "No," "Yes," and "We cannot know!"

- Why is there so much distress, anxiety, violence, and unhappiness in the world?
- To what extent must we suffer?
- Is there value in suffering?
- Can we develop mastery of our own thoughts, emotions, and actions?
- What does it mean to live the life of a moral man or woman?
- What is virtue and how can we acquire it?
- What do we owe to others—to our spouse, our family, our city, our nation, to all of humanity?
- Is there a God?
- If so, what is God's nature?
- Does God care about us?
- What is the greatest gift He has given us?
- What might we owe Him?
- What is the good life, and how do we obtain it?
- What leads to happiness?
- How can philosophy render us "invincible"?

It is answers to questions like these that those ancient Greeks seeking after wisdom attempted to find by stretching human reason to its limits and applying its conclusions within their daily lives—and they found some very good answers, answers that are as valid for keyboarding web-surfers today as they were for men and women perusing dusty unrolled parchments 2,000 years ago.

Lives, Lessons, Legacies

Let's really dig in to the nature of this book. "What kind of book is this? What's in it? Why was it written?" Good questions. Now, it's time for the answers. This book aims to inform and excite you about the four most prominent ancient Greco-Roman Stoic moralists: Gaius Musonius Rufus, Epictetus, Lucius Anneas Seneca, and Marcus Aurelius Antoninus Augustus. That's why it's divided into four main parts. (The ancients would have called the parts "books," so in that sense you are getting four books for the price of one.)

Lives. Since all four of these men considered philosophy not nearly so much a theoretical, academic discipline as a practical guide to living a good life, their own *lives* bear witness to the fruits of their philosophical contemplation. Hence, both to set the stage for an understanding of their teachings and to get a glimpse of their teachings in action, chapters 1, 4, 7, and 10, the first chapter for each of our Stoics, will provide mini-biographies, examining the fascinating lives of these very different men—from the philosopher, to the slave, to the rich attorney and imperial adviser, to the emperor himself, the most powerful man in the world. As different as they were, they taught very similar lessons.

Lessons. Once the stage has been set for their teachings, we will let these great teachers let loose their great *lessons* in chapters 2, 5, 8, and 11. With just a bit of commentary here and there, I will mostly let them speak for themselves, providing terse summaries in plain modern English of some of the Stoics' most profound and most practical teachings.

As for Musonius Rufus, unfortunately, the surviving remnants of his writings are very sparse and have been passed down only through later secondary sources; but fortunately, that provides me with the space in chapter two to provide a fairly thorough rendering of all twenty-one of his extant lectures, covering everything from how we should employ logic to how we should treat women, grow our families, decorate our homes, and shave (or not) our heads and our beards. Musonius is a wonderful voice of reason and sanity, and I suspect some readers will be quite surprised to see how some of his reason-based social teachings on sexuality, marriage, and family, for example, would not seem out of place within the pages of the *Catechism of the Catholic Church.*

There is much more material to work with when it comes to Musonius's most renowned student, Epictetus. Here, in chapter five, I will condense and present the fifty-three already-terse "chapters" summarizing his thought contained in his famous *Enchiridion* (literally Manual or Handbook, meaning "ready at hand" in the Greek). Epictetus is in many ways the Stoic's Stoic, the Stoic *par excellence* who lived and breathed Stoicism every day of his life in the role of a full-time philosopher; and I'll do my best to convey to you his true excellence in inspiring us to live lives of joy and virtue with peace in our hearts and harmony with our neighbors—and in showing us just how to do it.

A vast corpus of Seneca's writings survive, thanks be to God! My work is cut out for me in chapter eight to pick and choose a few handfuls of gems to share from the amazingly rich literature of this amazingly rich man—rich in wealth, in expression, in humanity, and in wisdom. His teachings on the value of philosophy for every one of us, on the nature of human emotions and how they naturally develop and how they can be artfully controlled, and on the true meaning of universal brotherhood, are but a few of the gems we will mine from his one-hundred twenty-four famous *Letters to Lucilius,* as well as his essays on topics ranging from *Anger* and *Clemency* to *The Good Life* and *Leisure,* and more.

And as for the final "lessons" chapter, number eleven, we will meditate upon the wisdom of the great Roman Emperor Marcus Aurelius through the twelve books of his *Meditations* that history has so kindly preserved for us. Here we will see an actual Caesar, and one of the last of the great ones, giving God His due in his most noble written musings to himself about how to live in accordance with nature, with a heart filled with gratitude, ready to bear insults and injuries without retribution, returning them instead with noble service to all humankind.

Legacies. The last of the three chapters (3, 6, 9, and 12) for each of our Stoics are where we'll examine their *legacies.* How have their ideas been received over time? How have they influenced Western culture as a whole? How have they influenced medieval and modern literature? How did they give birth to highly effective modern cognitive psychotherapies? And as our special focus (where "the Cross" of our title comes in) we will recall that Christ too taught lessons for life (indeed, for eternal life) and sometimes even from the porch, not of a Greek, but of the great Jewish Temple in Jerusalem.[3] We will examine how the some lessons of these great Roman Stoics hinted at teachings spelled out by Christ, how the Stoics and their ideas were received by the early Church Fathers, and how they have influenced Christian thought over the millennia. Most importantly of

3. See for example this book's beautiful cover image, by French artist Jacques Joseph "James" Tissot (1836–1902).

all, we will examine how their most enduring ideas can help *us* live better, more loving lives as Christians *today.*

Out from the Porch and into the World

The real nature of this book, if it is true to its purpose, should reflect the main goals of the Stoics themselves. It should inspire us to live out the great Stoic lessons in our own lives, creating legacies of practical wisdom through our families, friends, co-workers, fellow parishioners, neighborhoods, communities, and all who fall within our spheres of influence. It should instill a love of wisdom; a love of the ultimate source and fount of all wisdom; a desire to seek the truths that truly matter the most; a desire for virtuous, honorable living that brings the wisdom of the ancient painted porch into every modern living room. Let's go, then, without further delay to the first philosopher on the first porch.

PART I

Musonius Rufus: Profound Pro-Life Philosopher

✝

What a great spectacle it is when a husband and wife with many children are seen with their children crowded around them! No procession conducted for the gods is as beautiful to look at, and no ritual performed solemnly for a sacred occasion is as worthy of being watched, as is a chorus of many children guiding their parents through the city, leading them by the hand or otherwise caring for them. What is more lovely than this spectacle? What is more worthy of emulation than these parents, especially if they are decent people? What other people would we join with so eagerly in praying for good things from the gods? What other people, indeed, would we help obtain whatever they might need?

⁓Musonius Rufus, Lecture 15[1]

---

1. *Musonius Rufus: Lectures and Sayings*, trans. Cynthia King (CreateSpace.com, 2011), 63.

1

The Life of
the Roman Socrates

*Musonius Rufus was a 1ˢᵗ-century Roman philosopher of impressive
personality and nobility of character—"The Roman Socrates"—who
lived the virtuous life that he taught.*

J. T. Dillon[1]

WE KNOW PRECIOUS LITTLE about the man many modern scholars
have graced with the title "The Roman Socrates." He didn't write an
autobiography; indeed, like Socrates and Jesus Christ, he does not
appear to have left any writings at all. What we know of his life and
the lessons he taught comes in fragments from second-hand
sources, from students, historians, philosophers, and theologians
from his own time and from centuries later; but thank God and
those men for these precious fragments! The little that has come
down to us about Gaius Musonius Rufus makes it perfectly clear
that he is ever so much worth knowing, so let's get to know him as
best we can before we dig into his lessons.

At some time, most likely between the years 20 and 30 BC, during
the reign of Tiberius Caesar, there was born to a knight named Cap-
ito a son he would name Gaius Musonius Rufus. He was born in the
Etruscan city of Volsinii, most likely the site of the modern city of
Bolsenia, Italy, about 70 miles north and slightly west of Rome. He

---

1. J. T. Dillon, *Musonius Rufus and Education in the Good Life: A Model of Teaching and Living Virtue* (Dallas: University Press of America, 2004), 35.

would go on to live and teach in Rome, and while exiled, in Greece, for a time even upon the rocky slopes of Gyara, a desolate island of less than nine square miles in area in the Cyclades chain to the southeast of the Grecian mainland, surrounded by the wavy and "wine-dark"[2] Aegean Sea.

A Life of Exile

Little can be said of Musonius's early or later life. The Roman historian Tacitus reports in his *Histories* that Musonius was born into the class of equestrian knights, a rank just below the senatorial, implying significant social status and some measure of wealth, as well as political influence. Musonius studied philosophy, mastered its principles, and came to be a respected teacher of Stoicism in Rome. He was lauded by some emperors (e.g., Vitellius in his lifetime and Julian centuries later) and exiled from Rome by others (namely, Nero—twice—and Vespasian).

Musonius's first exile came sometime between AD 60 and 62, when he joined his friend, the respected Stoic and outspoken senator Rubellius Plautus, who had been exiled to Asia Minor by a jealous Nero Caesar. In the year 62, when Plautus learned that Nero had pronounced his death sentence, he turned to his friend Musonius for advice on whether to fight or to flee. Musonius advised neither course and counseled his friend against living his last days in anxiety. He gave him the Stoic advice that death is only an apparent evil, and maintaining dignity and virtue while still alive is what is truly good. Plautus did not resist the arrival of the centurion who would carry his head back to Nero at Rome.

Musonius returned to Rome, where his fame as a teacher of grew. In fact, Tacitus would write of the splendor of his name (*"claritudio nominis"*) at that time in his famous historical *Annals*. The petty and envious Nero came to see the accomplishments of great men as threats to his own glory and renown, and in the year 65 he banished Musonius from Rome. Many legends accrued surrounding this second Neronian exile. It was said that Nero exposed Musonius to cru-

2. As one of the poet Homer's favorite expressions would have it.

elties in prison that would have killed a man without such Stoic fortitude. He was reportedly placed in hard labor, forced to help dig out the canal at the isthmus at Corinth in Greece. Musonius responded with the equivalent of whistling while he worked, happily conversing and philosophizing with those who came from far and wide to see the philosopher at his physical labors.

He was later banished to desolate rock island of Gyara, so dismal that one of Nero's predecessors, the often cruel-hearted Tiberius Caesar, twice intervened to have people banished to a less hostile place. It was said that the island had no fresh water; yet the resourceful Musonius discovered on it a fresh-water spring. (Perhaps his experience with the Corinthian canal had made him as accomplished a digger as he was a philosopher!) And even in Gyara his philosophy flourished, as students from all over the Roman Empire sought him out there for his company and counsel, and turned the desolate rock into a mini-Athens or -Rome.

By the year 68 the Romans had had enough of the cruel and vicious Nero and sought to depose and kill him. Nero discovered the plot and fled with the intention to kill himself, but without the nerve to do so, whereupon he ordered his secretary Epaphroditus[3] to run him through with a sword. The next year Musonius returned once again to Rome.

Things went quite well for a time under the short-lived reigns of Galba, Otho, and Vitellius, and during the first years of Vespasian's rule. In fact, when Vespasian exiled all philosophers from Rome in AD 71, Musonius was the only philosopher known to have been exempted. It wasn't too long, though, until sometime in the mid-70s Musonius faced his third and final exile, this time to Syria, by the order of Vespasian.

Some incidents of note during this period of exile include his friendship with the military tribune and subsequently famous historian Pliny the Younger. Pliny wrote that he loved and admired Musonius, who was the father-in-law of Pliny's close friend, the

---

3. Small world that it is, we'll come across Epaphroditus again in Part II, since it was he who had owned a bright young slave and sent him to study with Musonius before he set him free. The slave's name was Epictetus.

Stoic Artemidorus. Musonius had selected Artemidorus as husband for his daughter because of his virtuous character. Also of great interest and merit, it was during this time that Musonius made his failed public protest against the display of gladiatorial games in a theater in Athens that was used for religious ceremonies.[4]

As noted before, not much at all is known about Musonius's later life, though he is assumed to have died possibly as late as circa AD 100. One of his friend Pliny's *Epistles,* written in AD 101, implies that Musonius had died by that time.

A Life of Excellence

Musonius taught mostly in Greek, and one of his favorite themes, as well shall see in chapter 2, was the cultivation of virtue. The Greeks called it *arête,* or *excellence.* Musonius preached virtue in general, as opposed to vice, and he also championed the four classic cardinal virtues of *temperance* (self-control), *fortitude* (courage), *prudence* (practical wisdom), and *justice.*[5] He also lived them, as a brief look at a few episodes in his life will make clear.

The value Musonius placed on temperance, on moderation and self-control in the pursuit of pleasures, be they of food, of sex, of comfort, or of material things, rings clear in his extant teachings, and there are no reports that he failed to practice what he preached.

One simple example of his courage can be seen in his willingness to go into the enemy camp of the General Vespasian who sought to usurp the seat of Emperor Vitellius (and who in short order did.) Musonius was sent late in the year 69 to try to broker a peace by praising the blessings of peace and unity to war-hardened, blood-thirsty legions in the midst of a military mission that would give them great booty. Tacitus reports that Musonius was mocked by many and his mission was a failure. Yet it bespeaks his courage and his integrity.

---

4. As we will see in the chapters ahead, other prominent Stoics, like Seneca and Marcus Aurelius, were also no fans of the gladiatorial games.

5. *Sophrosyne, andreia, phronesis,* and *diakaiosyne* in the Greek.

As for Musonius's practical wisdom or prudence, we saw it illustrated in the days of his exile when he gave water to the thirsty of the island of Gyara through his ingenuity in finding a well; and while exiled from the world, through the fame of his philosophy, he brought the world to him.

There is also a very specific incident that nicely illustrates Musonius's practice of the virtue of justice. As we'll see in Part II, Musonius held that it was unbefitting for a philosopher to sue anyone who had injured him, and yet Musonius is known for prosecuting one very important lawsuit. The suit was over no injury to him, but rather a treacherous and extreme injury to one of his noble friends. The Stoic philosopher and powerful proconsul Publius Egnatius Celer had fabricated charges of treason against Musonius's honorable and innocent friend, proconsul of Asia, Barea Soranus. In the year 66 Nero condemned Soranus to death, and in the year 70, two years after Nero's death, Musonius initiated a public prosecution against Celer, that man who had sullied the Stoic name and unjustly shed Stoic blood.

What kind of a person was Musonius? Was this Stoic "laid-back," or was he a "stickler"? Aside from what we can gather from Musonius's own teachings, we get but glimpses of his powerful personality and unflagging integrity in the reflections of his most prominent student, Epictetus, whom we'll meet in this book's Part II. For now, let one brief sample suffice:

> Rufus used to say: "If you have time enough to praise me, then I know what I am saying is worthless." And after saying this, he went on to say things that caused each one of us who sat there to think that someone at some time had given him revealing information about us: he grasped our circumstances so well, and he placed our faults before our eyes so effectively. Students, the philosopher's school is a doctor's office. You must leave not pleased, but pained. You do not come in healthy: one of you hurt his shoulder, another has an abscess, another a fistula, another headaches. Am I to sit you down and tell you clever slogans and sayings so that you praise me as I leave, even though the shoulder is no better than it was, the head still hurts, and the abscess and fistula remain? Do young men leave home for these reasons and leave their parents,

friends, kinfolk, and small property so that they may yell "hooray" when you utter witticisms? Did Socrates do this, or Zeno, or Cleanthes?[6]

I'd gather from this reflection that Musonius was *not* quite so "laid-back." Yet note too his care and his love for his students, whom he seemed in some ways to know better than they knew themselves. Note also his zeal for improving them for their own good, with no desire to seek out or bask in acclaim. Acclaim he does deserve, though. I think you will come to agree as we follow his examples from Corinth and Cyara and dig right into his lessons. Prepare now for a surprisingly refreshing font of pure, clear, Stoic wisdom on learning, living, loving—and even dying.

6. Epictetus, *Discourses*, 3.23.29–32, as translated in King, 2011.

2

Lectures for
Learning, Living, and Loving

Just as there is no use in medical study unless it leads to the health of the human body, so there is no use to philosophical doctrine unless it leads to the virtue of the human soul.

~Musonius Rufus, *Lecture* 3[1]

✝

THE MOST EXTENSIVE extant collection of Musonius's writings consists of 21 *Discourses*, or lectures, collected by a contemporary of his named Lucius and extracted in the fifth century AD by the Greek Joanne Stobaeus. Cora Lutz provided an excellent English translation, originally published in 1947,[2] and Cynthia King published an equally fine, more modern translation in 2011.[3] Varying from just one page to five pages at the most in length, these brief essays may have captured the gist of Musonius's informal post-lecture elaborations of topics for his students. They provide precious insights into his philosophy and teaching methods and precious lessons in learning, living, loving, and yes, even dying, even for those in our day.

These lectures are not nearly as widely known as they should be. I'll do my small part here to change that by stepping almost entirely

1. King, 30.
2. The edition I was able to obtain: Cora Lutz, *Musonius Rufus Fragments* (New Delhi, India: Isha Books, 2013).
3. Op. cit.

out of the way, primarily merely summarizing, abridging, paraphrasing, and at times, briefly quoting Musonius himself as we take a whirlwind tour of all of the twenty-one lectures. As a committed student of a 13th-century scholastic philosopher who knew the Stoics well,[4] I'll ask for your forbearance, since I've reshaped each lecture topic into the form of a question. Perhaps, though, that's how they originally started out, as seekers of wisdom posed questions like these to their wise teacher, Musonius Rufus. Let's see what they might have asked and how he would have answered.

Lecture 1:
How Many Arguments Does It Take to Prove a Point?

This question calls to this psychologist's mind another pressing question: "How many psychologists does it take to change a lightbulb?" Answer: "Only one, but the lightbulb has to *want* to change." This silly modern jest may actually bear some relevance to Musonius's answer to our question in the first of his lectures. He states that a praiseworthy philosopher will guide his students to the truth with as few arguments or proofs as are necessary, indicating that the clearer and more persuasive one's arguments are the fewer will be needed. Sometimes perhaps only one argument (like one psychologist) will do to effect that change and make the light go on in the student's mind. Still, the student, like the light bulb, must want to change and have the capacity to do so.

Musonius declares that preparation is needed in order to grasp truths quickly and easily. The gods need no proofs or arguments at all, because everything is clear and certain to them.[5] Humans, however, need to be led to higher truths by starting from the simple,

---

4. St. Thomas Aquinas, author of the world's largest and greatest question-and-answer book, the *Summa Theologica*.

5. St. Thomas Aquinas would later argue that this applied to the knowledge of the angels. As purely spiritual beings, their thought-processes do not begin with the bodily senses and pass through steps of sensation, perception, understanding, and reasoning; they intuit truth instantaneously through a special illumination from God. God, who is Truth, knows all truth eternally.

plain things already within their ken. Further, those who are naturally more intelligent and who are better educated and trained will grasp truths that are not self-evident more readily with fewer arguments. Consider the moral truth that pleasure is not a good in itself (for every good is desirable, but not every pleasure is). This may be very hard to grasp for a child or an adult who has been pampered in every way, made soft and weak, and left with a sense of entitlement. Yet consider the rigorously trained Spartan child who once asked the great Stoic teacher Cleanthes if rather than pleasure, pain and toil were not what is truly good. Cleanthes was so pleased he responded with this verse from Homer: "Thou art of noble blood, dear child, so noble the words thou speakest."[6]

Even beyond the power of properly worded arguments, and properly prepared students, the true philosopher will argue most efficiently and best help others grow wise when the *actions* of his life bear witness to the truths about which he speaks.

Lecture 2:
Must We Train Ourselves to Be Good?

Perhaps I've already let the cat out of the bag by mentioning in the summary of Lecture 1 that education and training help people grasp with fewer arguments moral truths that are not self-evident, but Musonius's answer is more subtle than what first meets the eye. We expect only doctors to excel in care of the sick and only trained musicians to play their instruments flawlessly; and yet each and every one of us, regardless of our training or lack of it, is expected to behave morally, to obey the laws or face punishment. Every human person is born with an innate inclination toward goodness and nobility. The seed of virtue lies within every one of us. We were made to be good. Though Musonius does not state it here, it is clear from his other lectures that it is through the pursuit of and practice of wisdom that we can cultivate that little seed so that it grows into a towering oak of virtue.

---

6. *Odyssey* IV.6111, as cited in Lutz, 2013.

Lecture 3:
Should Women Study Philosophy?

"Absolutely!" declares Musonius. Women have received the same gift of reason from the gods that men have, the same senses, most of the same body parts, the same capacity to know right from wrong, and the same inclination to virtue. Women no less than men are pleased by good and just deeds and decry what is base and shameful. Why would it not be appropriate for women to seek to live honorably and learn how to do so? That is what philosophy is all about. Should not a woman be good like a man?

A woman should have the practical *prudence* to manage a household or a state. She must be *self-controlled* to remain free from sexual improprieties, to avoid being argumentative, extravagant, vain, or a slave to her desires, so that she can control anger, persevere through grief, and become stronger than any emotion that seizes her. Any person, man or woman, who has studied and practiced philosophy will display such a beautiful character. A woman who studies philosophy will become *just* as well. A female philosopher would be a just and blameless spouse, co-worker, and mother, thinking it worse to commit a wrong than to suffer one, who would rather suffer with less than be greedy for more, who would love her children more than life itself. It is appropriate as well for a woman to obtain the *courage* that training in philosophy brings. She will not bow down to the powerful and mighty, but will nurse and protect the children she brings forth, stand firm by her husband, and will not shrink due to haughtiness from work others might say is fit for only slaves.

Some said the study of philosophy might lead women to become haughty, quarrelsome, and frivolous, abandoning their proper duties, seeking out arguments or dissecting syllogisms in the marketplace, when they should be sitting at home spinning wool. Musonius said such actions are unworthy in men as well. True philosophical discussion is conducted for the sake of practical application. Women should do this just as men should, and neither should abandon their duties to do it.

Here Musonius comes to the passage we quoted to start this chapter: "Just as there is no use in medical study unless it leads to the health of the human body, so there is no use to philosophical doctrine unless it leads to the virtue of the human soul." Philosophy is powerful medicine for the soul, good for what ails both men and women. So, yes!—women should study philosophy. Musonius concludes: "The doctrine of the philosophers encourages a woman to be happy and to rely on herself."[7]

Lecture 4:
Should Daughters Be Educated Like Sons?

Perhaps you have guessed from the lecture above where Musonius is going with this. Contrary to the common Greco-Roman wisdom of his day, Musonius answers our fourth question with another yes. Trainers of dogs and horses don't make distinctions in their training of males and females for the tasks they are to do, and neither should educators make distinctions in training human boys and girls in their main task of life, the acquisition of virtues. There are not separate sets of virtues for men and for women. Both must be sensible and just. Eating or drinking too much from a lack of self-control will be as shameful in a woman as it is in a man. Women need to be brave as well, and would not want to be inferior even to hens and other female birds that fearlessly do battle with any larger animal that threatens their chicks. Remember also the armed Amazon warriors. If some women lack courage, it's not from their lack of natural endowment, but from their lack of practice.

Philosophy provides such practice for courage and for all the virtues; so as far as the virtues are concerned, sons and daughters should have the same education. Some will then ask if men should spin wool with the women and women should pursue the same gymnastics as men. Musonius does not advise this. He notes that some tasks, because of innate differences in the builds and the bodily strength of men and women, tend to be better suited to each sex, which is why people have traditionally spoken of "men's work" and "women's work"; but even here there may be exceptions. He is talking about equal education for both sexes in the things that matter the most—like learning what is helpful and what is harmful,

7. King, 30.

what should be done and what should not, how to endure hardships, how to overcome fear of death, how to discern what is honorable and what is base and shameful. No man is properly educated without philosophy—and no woman is either. Women, like men, should develop good character and practice noble behavior, "since indeed philosophy is nothing but the practice of noble behavior."[8]

Lecture 5:
Is Practice More Important Than Theory in the Pursuit of the Good Life?

We now come to a point of the greatest importance to all four of our Greco-Roman Stoic moralists. To put it in a nutshell (well, three actually), Musonius poses three questions:

• If you were ill, would you prefer the help of a doctor who can speak brilliantly about the art of medicine, but who has not treated sick people, or of a doctor who cannot speak very well about medicine, but who is experienced in healing according to proper medical theory?
• Who would you hire as your captain, a man who has never piloted a boat, but can speak authoritatively on naval theory, or a man who can hardly put two words together, but has successfully sailed many ships?
• Who would you hire to perform, a musician learned in musical theory who cannot play an instrument, or one who knows no theory, but plays a mean cithara or lyre?[9]

Musonius assumes your answer in each case would be the person who has actual experience, the one who can clearly practice his craft effectively, regardless of his capacity to preach. He applies this as well to philosophy, asking if it clearly isn't better to be self-controlled and prudent than to be able to discourse about theories of temperance and prudence. Practice wins out over theory in philoso-

8. Ibid., 33.
9. Both are ancient variants of the harp. (Please feel free to substitute for these examples a piano and a harpsichord, an electric guitar and a tuba, or whichever musical instruments suit your fancy.)

phy because while *understanding* the theory behind virtuous actions enables one to *speak about* them, it is the *practice* of virtue that enables one to *act* virtuously. Theory is not without value, however, when it teaches one how to act and logically informs and comes before practice. Practical application should be in harmony with theory, but practice is more effective in leading people to action.

Lecture 6:
How Does One Practice Philosophy?

It is one thing to *know* what the virtues of self-control, justice, courage, and wisdom are, and quite another thing *live* them. Anyone who claims to seek wisdom through philosophy must practice more fervently than one pursuing the art of medicine or any other specialized skill, because philosophy is of greater importance and difficulty than any other pursuit. *Philosophy is the very art of living.* How, then, does one practice and train?

We must train according to the nature of what we are. Humans are a composite of body and soul, and both of these must be trained. Most attention should be directed to the higher part of the soul, but some care should also be given to the body, lest one should be lacking in his full humanity.[10] The philosopher must train his body in the capacity for virtuous work. The body is virtue's instrument or tool. We train both body and soul when we discipline ourselves to withstand cold, heat, thirst, hunger, small portions of food, and hard beds, to avoid pleasure and endure pain with patience. The first step in training the soul is to make sure that the proofs of what things are truly good and evil are always ready at hand,[11] and to

10. Cf. 1 Timothy 4:7–8: "Train yourself in godliness; for while bodily training is of some value, godliness is of value in every way, as it holds promise for the present life and also for the life to come."

11. John Sellars, in his *The Art of Living: The Stoics on the Nature and Function of Philosophy* (London: Bristol Classical Press, 2009), 130, notes that for the Stoics, keeping principles at hand implies even memorizing them, so they are always "at hand" for the mind. In Part II of this book, we will explore Musonius's most famous student, Epictetus, and his Enchiridion, literally "Handbook," of pithy Stoic wisdom well worth memorization.

accustom oneself to always distinguish truly good things from things that may appear good but are not. The next step is to train one's thought, so to speak, never to run from what appears evil but is truly good, nor to seek out what only appears to be good while avoiding true evils and seeking true goods. All in all, a person practicing philosophy will seek to master himself, to overcome both pleasure and pain, and to avoid clinging to life at all costs from a fear of death, and, in the case of goods or money, will not value receiving over giving.[12]

Lecture 7:
What Should We Make of Pain and Hardship?

Not too much, according to Musonius. Consider, he says, the hardships and dangers people endure to obtain ignoble things like illicit love, exorbitant profit, or fleeting flame. Should not we be willing to endure so much more in pursuit of things truly good? Is it not more worthy of our efforts, instead of winning our neighbor's wife, to rein in our desire for her? Rather than toiling endlessly for ever more wealth, isn't it better to train oneself to be satisfied with little? Instead of striving for notoriety, isn't it better to care not for fame and applause? In lieu of working to deprive our neighbor of what we envy, why not strive to envy no one? No one attains virtue without pain and hardship. The person who is unwilling to exert himself and suffer pain in pursuit of the good renders himself unworthy of it. "These words and others like them he then spoke, exhorting and urging his listeners to look upon hardship with disdain."[13]

Lecture 8:
Should Kings Study Philosophy?

Once a king from Syria came to Musonius and asked him if philosophy was a pursuit worthy of kings. Musonius explained that a king must be able to protect and benefit his people, knowing right from

12. Cf. Acts 20:35: "It is more blessed to give than to receive."
13. Lutz, 28.

wrong and justice from injustice; showing self-control, courage to face all enemies, knowledge and felicity of speech to confound those who contradict him, and a fatherly benevolence, like mighty Zeus himself. It is philosophy that teaches these things to a king and that makes every person, as Socrates said, king-like within his own realm.[14] Overjoyed with Musonius's reply, the king offered him whatever gift he would request. Musonius replied, "The only favor I ask of you is to remain faithful to this teaching, since you find it commendable, for in this way and no other will you best please me and benefit yourself."[15]

Lecture 9:
Is Exile an Evil?

For readers who recall Musonius's brief biography in chapter 1, it may come as no surprise that this is the lengthiest of Musonius's extant lectures, about five pages' worth. This noble man who thrice experienced exile at the whim of capricious emperors answered this question with a "No!"[16] Does exile deprive us of water, earth, air, the sun and other planets, or even of human company? Did not Socrates say that the universe is the common fatherland of all men? No one place is the cause of our happiness or unhappiness. As Euripides said,

> As all the heavens are open to the eagle's flight,
> So all the earth is for a noble man his fatherland.[17]

Industrious people in exile can find what they need to meet their basic needs and to flourish; and as for the things that matter the most, there is nothing about exile that prevents a person from exercising courage, justice, self-control, wisdom, or any of the virtues that bring honor and benefit to him and those around him. We see

14. The first of many references to the wisdom and example of Socrates, an ideal sage for the Stoics.
15. Lutz, 36.
16. While today few of us are exiled or banished against our will, many of us are required to spend extended time away from home, be it for school, work, a military tour of duty, or perhaps a permanent move to another city.
17. Cited in Lutz, 38.

many examples of this: for instance, in the exiles of Homer's Odysseus and of Diogenes of Sinope.[18] Musonius himself reminds his hearers that though an exile himself, no one ever heard him moaning or groaning! Indeed, he repeatedly said such things to himself to make the most good of his exiles.

Lecture 10:
Should Philosophers File Lawsuits?

No, they should not, according to Musonius Rufus; not for personal injuries, anyway. "If a philosopher cannot bear blows or jeering, he is useless. . . . A philosopher who thinks it right to forgive someone who offends him and acts accordingly is obviously better than one who thinks he must defend himself. . . ."[19]

Lecture 11:
What Is the Best Occupation for a Philosopher?

Perhaps you've guessed it's not a lawyer[20]—but did you guess that it's a farmer? The life of the farmer is noble and heaven-blessed. It is better to care for oneself than to have to ask someone else to meet one's needs; and nature is so generous in repaying many-fold those who carefully cultivate it that a hard-working farmer can support not only himself, but his wife and his family too. Some might disdain such physical labor as cultivating the land or herding flocks of sheep; but his flocks did not keep Hesiod from being among the greatest of poets. Farming need not interfere with philosophy, as one can think and discuss while working as well as during periods of rest. Indeed, perhaps the ideal school of philosophy would be that of the farm, with students working and conversing right alongside their teacher, hearing about self-control, courage, or justice while

18. As briefly mentioned in the preface, Diogenes, along with Socrates, was an honored hero of the Stoics.

19. King, 50. Cf. Matt. 5:39: "But I say to you, Do not resist one who is evil. But if any one strikes you on the right cheek, turn to him the other also."

20. Not to condemn all lawyers and lawsuits! Recall from chapter 1 that Musonius himself did prosecute one lawsuit, not for a crime against him, but for a crime that lead to the death of a dear friend.

performing arduous, virtuous work. After all, "those who want to do philosophy properly do not need many words."[21]

Lecture 12:
What Does Philosophy Have to Do with Sex?

Everything. Our sexual behaviors are to be in accord with reason and with nature; and it is philosophy that guards us against the luxurious living that seeks out all manners of illicit, unnatural sexual acts. Only those sexual acts carried out within the bonds of marriage and for the procreation of children are in accord with nature and reason. The worst sexual aberrations are those of adultery and of homosexual relations, which are unnatural acts. All unlawful sexual acts come from a lack of shame and of self-control. Some say that sexual relations with an unmarried woman or a slave girl cause no harm because they do not deprive anyone of their legitimate offspring—and yet, setting aside even the injustice to the female, and assuming that other parties are not injured, the person who acts basely debases himself, acting like a pig who relishes rolling in its own filth. In reply to the men who point out that owners legally claim the deed even of the bodies of their slaves, and that sex with them is not unlawful, Musonius asks whether, if it is not shameful or unlawful for a master to consort with a female slave, it should not be just as well for a master's wife to consort with a male slave. Should not men be capable of living up to the standards that they expect of women? Philosophy, then, has everything to do with sex, for it studies and fosters self-control in accord with nature.

Lecture 13:
Why Get Married?

The primary purpose for union in marriage is so that a husband and wife will live their lives together with the intention of having

---

21. King, 53. Cf. Musonius's first lecture on efficient argumentation, and perhaps as well in this context the saying often attributed to St. Francis Assisi: "Preach the Gospel always, and if necessary use words."

children. They will also consider all their possessions to be held in common between them, with nothing a private possession between them, not even their bodies. The child that results from their union is of the greatest importance, but is not the only important thing, since procreation can take place outside of marriage, as it does in the animal world. In marriage there must be above all companionship and mutual love between man and wife, indeed "both in health and in sickness and under all occasions, since it was the desire for this as well as for having children that both entered upon marriage."[22] If a spouse should ignore the meaning of marriage and focus only on his individual concerns, living in the same house but focusing on matters outside of it, the union will be destroyed or will result in a relationship worse even than loneliness. When spouses do share in perfect love and strive to outdo one another in their devotion to the other, their union is ideal and a thing of great beauty. Therefore, in choosing a spouse, one should neglect wealth, physical beauty, or high birth, and seek a mate of normal appearance, capacity for physical labor, and virtuous character.[23]

Lecture 14:
Does Marriage Hinder Philosophy?

When someone said to Musonius that a wife would seem to get in the way of the study of philosophy, Musonius answered (to paraphrase), "Why not ask Pythagoras, Crates, or Socrates about that?" Three of the greatest of philosophers lived the married life. Philosophers teach people how to live in harmony with nature, and if anything is in accordance with nature, marriage most clearly is. Indeed, if the Creator of mankind divided the human race into two sexes and instilled within our hearts a powerful longing for our counterpart, so too should a philosopher think beyond his own needs and

22. Lutz, 58.
23. History records that Musonius practiced what he preached in choosing as his daughter's spouse not a powerful, wealthy man within his social circle, but the philosopher Artemidorus, a man known for his virtue and for his humble manner of life.

act in the interest of his neighbor, creating a family, so that his entire city may flourish with homes full of citizens. Families and cities do not arise from men or from women alone, but from their blessed union. Indeed, "whoever destroys human marriage destroys the home, the city, and the whole human race."[24] A man should take thought of his own city and make his home a rampart to protect it. Married people serve more than themselves. They serve their spouses, their family, their neighbors, their cities. If these things are proper, then how can they conflict with the practice of philosophy? "After all, to practice philosophy is obviously to use reason to determine which actions are seemly and appropriate, and then to do them. This is how he spoke then."[25]

Lecture 15:
Why Is Abortion (and Contraception) Wrong?

Note how the ancient lawgivers, whose job it was to determine what was good for a city and what was bad, recognized that childbirth was good for their cities, and passed laws that promoted large families. "So it was for this reason that they forbade women to suffer abortion,"[26] and prescribe penalties for those who disobeyed. Indeed, "they forbade women from agreeing to be childless and from preventing conception, they honored married couples who had a lot of children, and they punished those who were childless."[27] To try to unnaturally limit the size of one's family is to act contrary to the wisdom of the ancient lawgivers and contrary to the will of Zeus, who guards the human race. One who is unjust to strangers sins against Zeus, the god of hospitality. One who is unjust to friends sins against Zeus, the god of friendship. One who is unjust to his own family sins against Zeus, the guardian of the family. Anyone who sins against the gods is impious.

24. Lutz, 62.
25. King, 61.
26. Lutz, 66.
27. King, 62.

Next, Musonius launches into the brief yet poignant paean to large families that was used as our epigraph to Part I of this book. After proclaiming the glories of a large family, Musonius addressed the excuse some would use, that they were too poor to raise a large family. Musonius responded: "But pray, whence do the little birds, which are much poorer than you, feed their young, the swallows and the nightingales and larks and blackbirds?"[28] Are not humans more intelligent and resourceful than the birds of the air? An even worse excuse than poverty for Musonius was that of those who would limit the size of their families so that the children born first would inherit greater wealth. Musonius went on to describe the many ways in which brothers are more valuable than wealth; and to claim that, indeed, we should strive to leave our children not many possessions but many brothers.

Lecture 16:
Must We Always Obey Our Parents?

Musonius believed that it is a good thing to obey our parents, but we should carefully examine just what it means to obey, first by examining what disobedience is. If a father who knew nothing of medicine prescribed something for his son that his son knew was harmful, it is not likely that he would be considered disobedient if he did not do what his father ordered. This is even clearer in a case wherein the father is sick and asks the son to bring him wine or some food that would make him more grievously ill. If the son knew this and denied his father's wishes, who would say this was true disobedience? Even less disobedient are the children of parents who would order them to steal, embezzle money, or commit even more heinous crimes. Indeed, Musonius personally knew of the father of a beautiful son who attempted to prostitute him. If the son had refused his father's demand, he asked, would the son be blameworthy for disobedience?

Regardless of who is issuing a command, be it a father, a ruler, or

28. Lutz, 68. (Cf. Matt. 5:26.)

even a dictator, if what is commanded is unjust there is no wrong in disobeying the command.[29] A disobedient person is one who disregards orders that are right, just, and noble, while the obedient person is just the opposite, one who willingly listens to and follows good and fitting advice. Indeed, there is a sense in which even the child who refuses what a parent commands because he knows it is harmful and wrong obeys his parent's wishes in a higher sense. How so? Because parents by nature should want what is best for their children, and if the child truly knows what is best in a particular situation, he should do what will lead to what is best for himself. "Anyone who wants to obey his parents in all of his actions need only consider whether what he intends to do is good and useful, and nothing else. If one follows this principle, he is obeying his parents."[30]

If a father should prohibit his child from studying philosophy, the child should first try to convince the father through reason of the good that philosophy brings; and whether or not he comes around, the child should treat him as a student of philosophy should, being courteous to him and helpful in every way. Real philosophers need always simply focus on doing what is right.

Lecture 17:
What Do Old People Need Most?

An old man once asked Musonius what the best way of life for the old was. He said it is the same way of life that is best for youth as well, to live life guided by the right principles in accord with nature. This is achieved by realizing that man was not created for pleasure, and indeed neither are horses, or cows, or dogs. We would think little of such creatures if they simply ate, drank, and mated all the time while doing none of the things that are the proper work of their species. They would fall short of their potential excellence, as

29. It is partly because of statements like these that Musonius and other Roman Stoics sometimes provoked the suspicion of the emperors, prompting their banishments of philosophers from Rome or from all of Italy.

30. King, 66.

all the more would such a man. It is the nature of each creature that determines its virtue or excellence, and it is the nature of man and of man alone to have been created in the image of God. God is the possessor of the virtues: intelligence, high-mindedness, justice, kindliness, and all others. He is stronger than desires, knows no envy, and loves and cares for all humankind.

There are some old people whom we call godly and holy, who have acquired these God-like virtues through a lifetime of proper education and practice. They endure their lost youth with no regret, have patience with the young, do not despair from their body's decline, and do not complain when others overlook them and their friends and relatives neglect them, because they have within their minds the antidote for all such things, the fruits of their past training. Indeed, they are even free from fear of death, since they never forget that it is every mortal's lot. Those who spend a lifetime in pursuit of true wisdom, learning what is truly good and what is truly evil, would not consider death, the necessary end to even a good life, as something that is evil.

Some think that wealth is the greatest consolation of old age; but there are many elderly rich people who are filled with sadness and despair. Again, the best consolation in old age is to live a noble life in accordance with our highest nature.

Lecture 18:
What Has Food to Do with Philosophy?

A great deal, according to Musonius Rufus, who spoke frequently and fervently on this topic that he considered no small matter for any philosopher. Musonius believed that habits of eating and drinking either build up or tear down the very foundation of the virtue of temperate self-control. There's an old adage advising would-be brides that "the way to a man's heart is through his stomach." For Musonius, the way to a man's or a woman's self-control is through his or her esophagus and stomach! "Indeed the throat was designed to be a passage of food, not an organ of pleasure, and the stomach was made for the same purpose as the root was created in plants. For just as the root nourishes the plant by taking food from without, so the stomach nourishes the plant by taking food and drink which are taken into it."[31]

Musonius expounds at great length in this two-part lecture on the proper approach to food. I will save many of the details for our next chapter, since it will bear directly on how ancient Church Fathers and medieval scholastic theologians would come to explain the nature and varieties of the sin of gluttony. For now I'll simply supply his summation: "To sum up the question of food, I maintain that its purpose should be to produce health and strength, that one should for that purpose eat only that which requires no great outlay, and finally that at table one should have regard for a fitting decorum and moderation, and most of all should be superior to the common vices of filth and greedy haste."[32]

Lecture 19:
How Should We Build Our Houses and Dress Ourselves?

After talking about food, Musonius goes on to talk about protecting the body from the elements, through clothing and through housing. Clothing should modestly cover the body and not be expensive or ostentatious. Indeed, footwear and clothing should function like armor, protecting the body, not putting it on display. Further, one should not coddle the body and make it weak through excessive layers or soft materials. It is a good and toughening thing to experience some cold in the winter and some heat in the summer.[33] If possible, one should go without shoes or sandals, which are not unlike shackles. It is good for the feet to move freely. Indeed, in Musonius's day, neither couriers nor competitive runners would be seen wearing sandals as they went through their paces or raced in their races.

As for housing, it too should serve to protect rather than to display. The philosopher has no need for fancy colonnades, prettily

31. Lutz, 88.
32. Ibid., 90.
33. I shudder to think what Musonius would think of those among us today who would never deign to buy a car without built-in seat and steering-wheel warmers!

painted rooms, or costly inlaid floor tiles. Such things are expensive, and the money could be better spent, for example, helping others in need. Indeed, it is more worthwhile to build a big circle of friends than to build a big house.

Lecture 20:
How Should We Furnish Our Homes?

Once one's house is built, similar principles apply to how it should be furnished. In fact they can be reduced to three: *acquisition, use,* and *preservation.* One's furnishings should not be obtained at great cost and difficulty; they should be well-suited to their function, easy to maintain and unlikely targets of theft. Take something as simple as cups. Earthenware cups can be acquired at the smallest fraction of the cost of silver or golden ones, serve just as well to hold wine (and indeed do so even better, since precious metals can taint the taste of wine), and are far less likely to be coveted by thieves.

Consider the ancient Spartans: raised for virtue in the most austere of environments, they were esteemed as the best of the Greeks. They made their very poverty more enviable than the wealth of the Persian King. Indeed, Musonius declared that he would rather suffer illness than live a life of luxury; for being sick harms only the body, but luxury harms both body and soul, weakening the body and giving rise to cowardice, covetousness, injustice, and lack of self-control within the soul.

Lecture 21:
Should Men Shave?

Bearing in mind that the beard was the philosopher's trademark in Musonius's time, we read that he declared that a man should shave his head or beard the way that a gardener prunes vines, merely to remove what is useless. The beard, says Musonius, is to a man what the crest is to the rooster or the mane to a lion! It is not useless, since it protects the chin and makes clear that its wearer is a man. Musonius's main point was that men should not expend unreasonable time and effort on grooming in order to beautify and draw attention to themselves.

From Lessons to Legacy

So we end our whirlwind tour of highlights from Musonius's 21 extant discourses on that last hairy note. Let's move on, then, to see what history has made of them; and, perhaps, how their wisdom can help us to remake ourselves.

3

A Legacy of Sanity
in Need of Rediscovery

And those of the Stoic school—since, so far as their moral teaching went, they were admirable, as were also the poets in some particulars, on account of the seed of reason [the Logos] implanted in every race of men—were, we know, hated, and put to death—Heraclitus for instance, and, among those of our own time, Musonius and others. For, as we have intimated, the devils have always effected, that all those who anyhow live a reasonable and earnest life, and shun vice, should be hated.

         ~ St. Justin Martyr, *Second Apology*, Ch. 8

For there are found in every philosophical sect, and in the word of God, persons who are related to have undergone so great a change that they may be proposed as a model of excellence of life. Among the names of the heroic age some mention Hercules and Ulysses, among those of later times, Socrates, and of those who have lived very recently, Musonius.

         ~ Origen, *Contra Celsus*, III. 66

Thoughtlessness is very close to insanity.

         ~ Musonius Rufus, *Lecture 21*

✝

IN MODERN WORKS by those who have not studied the Stoics' own writings or applied their principles within their own lives, the ancient teachers of the porch are often mentioned in passing as joyless, wooden, isolated masters of repression, lacking common sense and missing out on the joys and fullness of life. To study even the small remnants of the thoughts of Musonius Rufus clearly gives the lie to such misperceptions. Musonius provides for us a refreshing view and a clear voice of sanity. He sees things according to their nature, and gladly proclaims happy truths about what is good and what merely seems so. "Political correctness" was not in his vocabulary!

The Stoics were by no means self-absorbed individualists either. Their concerns extended to their families, neighborhoods, cities, and nations, to all of humankind, and indeed, all the way to the Creator of us all. We can see the profound respect for Musonius's personal integrity and philosophical sanity in philosophically astute early Christian theologians, including St. Justin Martyr (ca. AD 100–165), St. Clement of Alexandria (150–215), and Origen (184–254).

It is striking that of the little that has come down to us of Musonius's teachings, so much focuses on the duties and joys of family life, with many principles and exhortations that would not seem out of place in the modern *Catechism of the Catholic Church*. These views were not unique within the Stoic world, and we see them passed on and amplified particularly in the fragments from the Stoic Hierocles (2nd century AD). We know little about him, but some fragments of his teachings were preserved, as were those of Musonius, by Stobeaus (ca. 4th–5th centuries) in his *Florilegium* (or "*Anthology*").

In the preserved fragments describing *How We Ought to Conduct Ourselves to Our Kindred,* Hierocles describes a series of concentric circles, the first and smallest circumscribing one's self; the next-larger one, one's parents, siblings, spouse, and children; the next grandparents, aunts, uncles, nieces and nephews; the next remaining relatives, and on to ever widening circles encompassing one's city, its environs, on to one's province and one's nation, and lastly, to all of the world. Regarding these circles of kinship, we are to become aware of them and of all of their interconnections, striving to conduct ourselves benevolently and lovingly to all within each of the circles, indeed, striving to draw them all in closer to our innermost circle.

Hierocles writes most movingly when he describes the joys of marriage and parenthood and of what we owe to God. Indeed, he, like Musonius, was a profound, pro-life philosopher, employing the light of reason God has given to all men and women. When recounting the many reasons people should *not* abort or contracept, in a manner so foreign to ancient and modern reason-based arguments *for* abortion and contraception based only on *selfish* concerns, such as love of riches and fear of lacking the money to possess the material things of our dreams, Hierocles speaks of the joy that our parenthood brings *to the parents who gave us our life*:

> For the procreation of children is gratifying to them; because, if we should suffer any thing of a calamitous nature prior to their decease, we shall leave our children instead of ourselves, as the support of their old age. But it is a beautiful thing for a grandfather to be conducted by the hands of his grandchildren, and to be considered by them as deserving of every other attention. Hence, in the first place, we shall gratify our own parents, by paying attention to the procreation of children. And, in the next place, we shall cooperate with the prayers and ardent wishes of those that begot us. For they from the first were solicitous about our birth, conceiving that through it there would be a very extended extension of themselves, and that they shall leave behind them children of children, and have to pay attention to our marriage, our procreation, our nurture.[1]

Notice that for Hierocles, interaction between grandchildren and grandparents is "*kalos*," a "beautiful" thing. Indeed, he says the same of marriage between one man and one woman. And to those who would argue against bearing and raising children, Hierocles has this to say:

> *Moreover, it appears that every one who voluntarily, and without some prohibiting circumstance, avoids marriage, and the procreation of children, accuses his parents of madness, as not having engaged in wedlock with right conceptions of things.* It is easy to see, that such a one forms an incongruous opinion. For how is it possible that he should not be full of dissension, who finds a pleasure in living, and

---

1. Stobaeus, *Florilegium*, trans. Thomas Taylor (1822), 103. Text accessed at http://www.universaltheosophy.com/pdf-library/1822_Political-and-Ethical-Fragments.pdf.

willingly continues in a life as one who was produced into existence in a becoming manner by his parents, and yet conceives that
for him to procreate others is one among the number of things
which are to be rejected?[2]

The philosophy of ancient Stoicism, is, as we'll address in later
chapters, is making a resurgence today as a practical guide to living.
For now, I'll note that it remains to be seen to what extent the Stoic
embrace of the sanctity and beauty of marriage between one man
and one woman, and the fruits of their union in terms of large families, will ultimately be embraced or rejected in our time. Let's proceed with some quick commentary on a few other areas of
Musonius's lasting legacy, before we move examine the lessons that
were learned and taught in turn by his greatest student.

Lectures 1–11:
On Learning, Loving, and Living Philosophy

An old saying goes, "great minds think alike." When reading Musonius's first lecture, on the value of using a few practical and clear
arguments rather than many complicated ones to prove a philosophical point, I can't help but think of the first page of the Prologue to St. Thomas Aquinas's *Summa Theologica*, wherein Thomas
laments how students of the "sacred science" of theology have been
hampered by other authors "partly on the account of the multipli-
cation of useless questions, articles, and arguments. . . ." Indeed, he
concludes his Prologue with this remark: "Endeavoring to avoid
these and other like faults, we shall try, by God's help, to set forth
whatever is included in this Sacred Science as briefly and clearly as
the matter itself may allow."[3]

While we have more than 3,000 pages of what follows in St. Thomas's arguments in the *Summa Theologica* alone, only a few dozen
pages of Musonius's arguments remain for us, but precious they are.

2. Ibid., 104. Italics in the original.
3. St. Thomas Aquinas, *Summa Theologica* (Notre Dame: Christian Classics,
1981), prologue, xix.

How interesting that the great Stoic philosopher and the greatest Christian philosopher both sought out truth and endeavored to pass it on to others so that their lives might be transformed for the better, and that they started from similar premises.

We see Musonius's love for the powerful truths of philosophy in his second lecture, where he argues that God has placed the seeds of virtue in all of us. We need special training to be a doctor or a musician, for example; but God has given us all the capacity to distinguish right from wrong, and it is philosophy's role to develop this seed within us so that virtuous life may flourish. The Stoics did not know of Christ as the ultimate guide to a virtuous and ultimately everlasting life, and neither did they grasp the reality of original sin and of humanity's fall, since they had not received God's special revelation; but they did indeed grasp the lesson spelled out clearly in Genesis that all that God had made was good, very good,[4] and indeed, as Musonius would declare explicitly in Lecture 17, that man alone of all the creatures was made in the image of God.[5]

In his lectures endorsing the study of philosophy by women and the same fundamental moral training for girls and boys, we see that when Musonius states that "man" is made in the image of God, by "man" he most clearly and equally includes "woman."[6] Note as well that Musonius's fourth lecture espousing equal moral training of children of both sexes does not speak of the education of "girls" and "boys," but rather of "daughters" and "sons." Recall the Stoics' goal of living in accordance with nature, which requires the understanding of the nature of things, including human beings. Musonius does not speak of mere "girls" and "boys" but of "daughters" and "sons," because even here, in this lecture on education, he remembers human nature. He does not speak of abstract groupings of "gender," nor of young male and female citizens, as if owned by some state,

---

4. Genesis 1:10, 12, 19, 21, 25, 31.

5. Cf. Genesis 1:26–27: "Then God said, 'Let us make man in our image, after our likeness. . . .' So God created man in his own image, in the image of God he created him: male and female, he created them."

6. As the verse above from Genesis also makes crystal-clear.

but first and foremost of the fact that every girl or boy is someone's "daughter" or "son." Who more than a parent should care that their child is raised up in a way that will cultivate the seeds of virtue within them, and who is ultimately more responsible? Time and again Musonius's "family values" ring loud and clear through his lectures; and the way to best protect and promote family life per Musonius is through the pursuit of the cardinal virtues and the wisdom that embodied Stoic philosophy.

Lectures 5 and 6 make clear the value Musonius gave to the *practice* of philosophy, regarding this so much more highly than merely *knowledge* of philosophy.[7] The proof of a philosophy is in the pudding of actual virtuous lives lived out in accordance with reason and nature, bringing peace to the soul of the student of philosophy and expressing itself in benevolent deeds, enhancing the lives of all of those around him or her. Musonius does not by any means totally discount the role of knowledge and theory in living a life of virtue. We will better know what is truly good by a thoughtful search for the truth. But once a moral truth is found, it is far more important that is lived than that it is just learned.

Lectures 6 and 7 show how the philosophical life is worth any pains or hardships it may bring, to every single person, even to a king. Musonius is so on-target in describing the sad real-life stories of people seeking false goods (and perhaps false gods), like fool's gold of the allures of another's man wife, or of the foolish pursuit of real gold. Are not our entire modern advertisement and entertainment industries built precisely upon inspiring our lusts for such things? (Don't take my word for it, just turn on your television for five minutes or less during the next commercial break—or even during the program.) Philosophy offers something much harder, and much better: a life of dignity in pursuit of what matters the most, virtues like wisdom, self-control, courage, and justice. Indeed, a king needs such things more than anybody else; and even

---

7. Cf. James 1:22: "But be doers of the word, and not hearers only, deceiving yourselves"; and 1 John 3:18: "Little children, let us not love in word or speech but in deed and truth."

a pauper becomes like a king when he attains through philosophy mastery over himself.

The treasures philosophy brings are particularly valuable because, once attained and defended, they cannot be taken away. This we see in lectures 9 and 10. You can exile a philosopher from his home land, but you cannot banish from him his love of truth and virtue. Indeed, Musonius himself did not moan and groan in exile, but gladly worked on the ancient equivalent of a modern prison chain gang, conversing and philosophizing with his heart and soul while he dug with his arms and back. And as for personal insult, the true student of philosophy has nothing to lose from that. A philosopher, Musonius said, would not sue a man over a personal insult, because there is no shame in being insulted, but only in behaving in an insulting manner to another. No insult can harm a true student of philosophy. And even for physical injuries, Musonius cites the cases of philosophers who suffered physical attacks, and rather than plotting revenge and "biting back" as animals would do calmly bore the injuries and forgave their assaulters, much like He who, half a century earlier and 1,400 miles to the east, advised those who would follow him to "turn the other cheek."[8]

The last lecture we'll consider in this section, number 11, shows ever so literally how the philosopher seeks to live in accordance with nature, as Musonius declares that the life of a farmer, either of crops or of livestock, may be the ideal occupation for philosophers and for their students. Human art and effort perfects the bounty of nature. Philosophers who cultivate the land will be rewarded abundantly, not just in crops or in meat but in the growth of hard-won virtue and in the care of their families. Students of philosophy who would listen to their teachers as they jointly work the land and in periods of well-earned rest would obtain that kind of training in body and soul that Musonius so recommended.

8. Matt. 5:39.

Lectures 12–16:
On Learning, Loving, and Living Life

I would wager that it is these lectures that might most surprise modern readers, even well-read Christians and students of the Stoics, revealing how this ancient pagan Stoic philosopher, guided by God-given natural reason, became such a profound, pro-family, pro-life philosopher. Bullet-points below summarize some of Musonius's most fundamental and striking statements on human sexuality, marriage, procreation, abortion, contraception, and large families, complete with comparative references to paragraphs within the modern *Catechism of the Catholic Church*.

• Only sexual acts carried out within the bounds of marriage and open to the procreation of life are morally right (Lecture 12; cf. *CCC* 2360–2366, 2390–2391).

• Among the most serious illegitimate sexual practices are adultery and homosexual acts. Both arise from lack of self-control, and homosexual acts are intrinsically opposed to nature (Lecture 12; cf. *CCC* 2380–2381, 2357–2359).

• The chief purpose of marriage is that a man and wife will live together and have children (Lecture 13; cf. *CCC* 2366–2367).

• Marriage is founded upon mutual love and care "in sickness and in health" (Lecture 13; cf. *CCC* 2360–2361—and traditional Christian wedding vows).

• The marriage bond of partnership and union is admirable and beautiful (Lecture 13; cf. *CCC* 2362).

• Anyone who works to destroy marriage destroys family, city, and the human race (Lecture 14; cf. *CCC* 2209–2211).

• Lawgivers were wise to prohibit abortion and methods of artificial contraception (Lecture 15; cf. *CCC* 2366–2367, 2370–2372, 2270–2275).

• Large families are great gifts from God (Lecture 15; cf. *CCC* 2373).

From this group of lectures we most clearly see that, as for John Donne 15 centuries later, for Musonius Rufus no man (and no woman) is an island. Every Roman Stoic was raised in a family and would agree with the words of the *Catechism* that "the family is the *original cell of social life*" (2207). We are all parts of the body of life and have no right to sever or prohibit the growth of other parts. Indeed, we will find personal fulfillment when we do our best to make that body that gave life to us continue to grow and thrive. We are also morally bound to honor our parents and to obey them unless they issue commands contrary to what we know is morally right. In this too we see the harmony of Musonius's sixteenth lecture with the modern *Catechism*, which informs us that "if a child is convinced in conscience that it would be morally wrong to obey a particular order, he must not do so" (2217).

Lectures 17–21:
On Preparing for Death

The last five of Musonius's surviving lectures start with consideration of the end of life. We saw that he said the most important thing for the aged is the same as the most important thing for the young, to live a life of virtue in accordance with reason and nature. As for death, one who nears it in old age should recall that it is the fate of all, both the wicked and the good, and that what necessarily follows even a good life cannot of itself be evil.

Here, of course, the way of the porch and the way of the cross, cross paths. Though different Stoics had varying thoughts on the possibility of an afterlife (addressed perhaps in greatest depth by Seneca), they did not know of Christ and of the life to come. As for *this* life, though, they had much good counsel to offer on living a good life in preparation for a good death. As the last few discourses on food, clothing, housing, and even shaving show, Stoicism was a practical philosophy for living a good life; therefore, even the most mundane and seemingly un-philosophical of topics were grist for the Stoical mill.

For example, Lucius, the scribe of Musonius's discourses, noted that Musonius thought that food was a very important topic and spoke about it quite frequently. Here, Musonius's wisdom presages in many ways the advice of the Christian who five centuries later popularized the famous list of the "seven deadly sins," Pope St. Gregory the Great. Gregory, in his *Moralia on the Book of Job*, listed

55

seven deadly sins: gluttony, lust, greed, envy, sloth, and vainglory.[9]
When St. Gregory, and later St. Thomas Aquinas, expounded upon
the varieties of the sin of gluttony, they described dangers of eating
too much food, too-expensive food, too-daintily-prepared food,
and of eating too quickly or eating too often. St. Thomas cited an
old medieval verse that summed up the various forms in which
gluttonous behaviors are expressed: "*hastily, sumptuously, too much,
greedily, daintily.*"

We find these concerns in Musonius's eighteenth lecture as well.
He warns of the gluttony of eating more than we should; of eating
luxurious, gourmet foods, indeed, of "wallowing in the pickles and
sauces"; of being a picky eater; of preferring sweet foods to healthy
ones; of eating greedily and at "unseasonable times." He minces no
words, and warns us that gluttony makes us more like pigs or dogs
than rational human beings.

And here is where our great Stoic philosopher and our great
medieval Catholic theologians share an even more important common ground on gluttony. Gregory states in his *Moralia* that "unless
we tame the enemy dwelling within us, namely, our gluttonous
appetite, we have not even stood up to engage in the spiritual com-
bat." Musonius, 500 years before him, also saw gluttony as a gateway
sin of sorts. The temptations of gluttony are before us every day, and
if our powers of self-control are eroded through gluttony they will
not rise to the challenge in other more important areas of our lives.
For the great Catholic theologians, gluttony is a turning-away from
the true good of God for the sake of lesser goods that can do our
bodies harm; and our foundational Roman Stoic held virtually the
same view. Citing Socrates before him, who said we should eat to
live rather than live to eat, Musonius counseled a moderate intake of
simple, inexpensive, natural, healthy foods. (No wonder he thought
the best job for a philosopher was that of a farmer!)

9. Pride is often included in the list instead of vainglory. Gregory, like St. Thomas Aquinas after him, included vainglory among his seven, identifying pride as a
yet more profound sin, one that gives rise to the deadly sin of vainglory and to all
the others.

The same Stoic principles are applied to clothing, housing, fur-furnishing, and even to shaving and grooming, in the last three of Musonius's lectures. He counseled modesty and simplicity over ostentatiousness, and functionality over display. Remember how Musonius said that a philosopher teaches more by his actions than by his words. Material things and pleasures are not the highest goods and should not be valued too greatly. The philosopher will bear this out in the simple manner of his own dress, home, and possessions. Musonius presages the great impact that Saints Dominic and Francis, founders of the Orders of Preachers and of the Friars Minors, respectively, would make twelve centuries down the road when they preached the gospel of Christ more effectively than jewel-encrusted secular bishops, from within the simple robes that witnessed to their vows of material poverty.

One Last Fragment Sets the
Stage for Musonius's Greatest Student

It may seem a bit of a letdown to discover that our last surviving discourse from Musonius is about something as mundane and simple as the philosopher's hair and beard; but we must recall that we've been blessed only with remaining snippets—the clippings, we might say, of the great bearded philosopher's lessons. However, we are also privy to over fifty very brief sayings or fragments of Musonius as preserved in the works of later writers. I'll end with just one from Stobaeus's *Saying* 38, which he indicates is from Epictetus, who in turn attributed the words to his teacher, Musonius Rufus. They breathe the breath of the core of practical Stoic philosophy, of the basis of our capacity to reshape our lives in harmony with nature and reason. You will see two chapters down the road how Epictetus took these words from his master and ran with them like none before or since:

> Of the things that exist, Zeus has put some in our control and some not in our control. In our control is the most beautiful and important thing, the thing because of which even the god himself is happy—namely the proper use of impressions. Such use brings

freedom, prosperity, serenity, and stability; it also brings justice, law, self-control, and complete virtue.[10]

Musonius lists the first effect of the "proper use of impressions" as freedom. Next we turn to the philosopher who wrote most and best of the "proper use of impressions," the man who was born a slave and became one of the freest men who ever walked the earth, thanking God for his every step.

PART II

Epictetus:
God's Lame Messenger

✝

Why what else can I, a lame old man, do but sing hymns to God? If, indeed, I were a nightingale, I should sing as a nightingale, if a swan, as a swan. But as it is, I am a rational being, therefore, I must be singing hymns of praise to God. This is my task; I do it, and will not desert this post, as long as it may be given to me to fill it; and I exhort you to join me in this same song.

～ Epictetus, *Discourses* I.16 [1]

1. Oldfather, 111.

4

The Life of the Slave
Who Knew True Freedom

He was a man who relied wholly upon himself and God, but not on Fortune. In origin low and servile, in body lame and feeble, and in mind most exalted, and brilliant among the lights of every age.... There is no one who better influences and shapes a good mind. I never read that old man without a stirring of my soul within me, and, as with Homer, I think more of him each time I re-read him, for he seems always new; and even after I have returned to him I feel that I ought to return to him once more.

 Justus Lipsius on Epictetus[1]

✝

MUCH THAT WAS SAID of Musonius Rufus could be applied also to his most illustrious student, Epictetus. They both lived lives of exile and of excellence. Both walked their talk and were men of the highest integrity. Neither man wrote anything for publication, let alone an autobiography. The nuggets of their wisdom that we do possess came originally from students who wrote down what they said during public discourses and informal discussions after formal lessons. Thankfully in the case of Epictetus, because of his devoted student, the historian Flavius Arrian, the golden nuggets are far bigger and far more numerous than those of Musonius, as they stand preserved in Arrian's concise *Enchiridion* ("*Manual*" or "*Handbook*") and in the four remaining books of his more elaborate *Diatribai* ("*Dia-*

---

1. 16th-century Flemish author of *On Constancy in Times of Public Evil*. Cited in Oldfather, v. 1, xxix.

tribes" or "*Discourses*"). We'll discuss those remaining works in our next chapter on Epictetus's lessons, with special emphasis on the condensed lessons of the *Handbook*. For, now, I will simply note that while our knowledge of the details of Epictetus's life make pretty slim pickings, the force and impact of his inimitable personality ring out loud and clear in the strikingly vivid episodes of the books of the *Discourses*.

In Arrian's introductory comments to his collection of Epictetus's writings, he reports that he tried to take down what Epictetus had said verbatim, capturing "his way of thinking and the frankness of his speech." He noted that Epictetus did not care if others despised his choice of words, because he uttered them "clearly aiming at nothing else but to incite the minds of his hearers to the best of things." Arrian apologizes if his writings do not produce the same effect: "but if not, let those who read them be assured of this, that when Epictetus himself spoke them, the hearer could not help but feel exactly what Epictetus wanted him to feel. If however, the words by themselves do not produce this effect, perhaps I am at fault, or else, perhaps, it cannot well be otherwise. Farewell."[2]

Let's now take a look at this man who was so worth hearing, who so focused on the best of things, who was so moving, and who has helped countless people fare well in the 1,900 years since his passing.

A Life of Slavery

Epictetus was born to a Greek slave woman around the year 55, during the reign of Emperor Nero, at Hierapolis, Phrygia (modern-day Pumakkale in the southwest of Turkey). We don't know the names of his parents, or even the name they gave him. "Epictetus" comes simply from the Greek word *epiktetos*, meaning "acquired"—like a slave. Extremely little is known of his youth, except that he was moved to Rome and for a time was owned by Epaphroditus, himself

---

2. Oldfather, v. 1, 7, as are all quotations in this paragraph. They come in the form of Arrian's brief letter of greeting and introduction to Lucius Gellius, to whom he had sent the manuscript.

a former slave, a powerful personal secretary first to Nero and later to the Emperor Domitian.

Epictetus frequently calls himself a "lame old man," and a story often repeated in ancient writings relates that an owner (not necessarily Epaphroditus) intentionally twisted and broke Epictetus's leg. In fact, the story holds that Epictetus calmly told his owner in classic Stoic fashion that if he kept doing what he was doing his leg would break, and then indeed it did. Some scholars have questioned the story, noting that one ancient source, Suidas,[3] mentions that his leg grew lame from rheumatism. The story that a master broke it is preserved in the Christian writings of Origen and St. Gregory of Nazianzus. Simplicius, the sixth-century Platonist who wrote an extensive *Commentary on Epictetus' Encheiridion*, simply notes that Epictetus's leg was lame from a very young age. The 20th-century classicist W. A. Oldfather weighed in that while the cause of his lameness is not known, Epictetus clearly uses far more examples of bearing up to physical abuses from others than of bearing up to natural illnesses.

In any event, Epaphroditus apparently recognized Epictetus's rare intelligence, and he allowed him to study philosophy under Musonius Rufus. This was a total life-changer for Epictetus. Epictetus would soon after attain his freedom from slavery, and as a professional teacher of philosophy would become one of history's greatest champions of the internal, psychological freedom that comes only from self-mastery.

A Life of Freedom

We know that Epictetus was exiled from Rome sometime between AD 89 and 95, when Domitian exiled all philosophers from Rome and the entire Italian peninsula. Epictetus moved to Nicopolis, a large, thriving city on the western coast of Greece established in 28 BC by Gaius Octavius, the man who one year later began his 40-year reign as ruler of the world, bearing the title "Augustus Caesar."

---

3. The tenth-century author, possibly a Christian cleric at Constantinople, of a very influential lexicon or encyclopedia of ancient and medieval Greek learning.

The city was founded to celebrate his victory over Mark Antony in nearby Actium. The name Nicopolis means "City of Victory" in Greek. (I would aver that another man achieved a far more important and lasting victory there, a lame old man by the name of Epictetus!)

Nicopolis's seaside location made it an ideal spot for trade and commerce, and it was frequented by a great number of people traveling back and forth between Italy and Greece. In one of his lectures, Epictetus mentions his own "spies" who would travel to Rome to keep him informed of the goings-on there. Epictetus chose Nicopolis as the location where he would hang up his shingle and train up young men in virtue at his school of Stoic philosophy. He must have acquired a good reputation as a teacher, since it seems that his school thrived. Parents of means sent their children there. The *Discourses* mention various important persons who sought him out, and some sources report that the Emperor Hadrian (who reigned AD 117–138) also once paid him a call.

Though Epictetus was successful as a philosopher, he did not seek or acquire any great worldly wealth. He reportedly owned a small estate. His home was simple, his furnishings not much more than a pallet and a mat, and he never bothered to lock his door. He relates the story of the time a thief stole his iron lamp. He said it was a pity that the man would sell his dignity for the price of a lamp; as for Epictetus himself, he did have need for a lamp, so he simply bought a more homely earthenware one to replace it, one not too likely to inspire another thief's covetousness.

As for his family life, a story relates that one time while lecturing in public, Epictetus advised his students to marry and start families. A heckler then sarcastically asked the bachelor philosopher if he might have one of *his* daughters' hands in marriage! It appears, though, that later in life Epictetus followed his own marital advice, taking a wife to help him raise the child of a friend of his who had planned to expose it to die. He, like Musonius, defended fragile human life.

Epictetus's life was not particularly eventful from the outside observer's perspective. We can surmise from his descriptions of the gigantic statues of Athena and Zeus that he traveled to Athens and to Olympia; but he appears to have lived in Nicopolis the rest of his life, never returning to Rome. He cared not much for the naturalistic, scientific studies of his day, and his references to literature, mostly that of Homer, did not reveal a particularly wide learning. He clearly knew the writings of Plato and Xenophon, particularly those in which they reference Socrates, but it appears his main focus was on the then-massive and now mostly lost corpus of Stoic wisdom, the prolific works of Chrysippus.

Epictetus's words captured in the *Discourses* are memorable and endearing for their blunt and gruff forcefulness, and also for their earthy simplicity. They are rife with stories of happy, clapping children[4]; of mugs, pots, and lamps; of boxers, wrestler, runners, pent-athletes, "mixed-martial artists"[5]; of fathers, doctors, fortune-tellers,[6] and politicians; of lions, wolves, foxes, horses, and hens; and also of rival philosophers. They abound in tongue-in-cheek hyperbole, exaggeration, and self-deprecating humor. In refuting Skeptics, for example, who would claim that we cannot be sure of anything, while gesturing he asks (to paraphrase), "Why then when they want to eat, do they always bring the food *here* and never *here!*"[7] He did not molly-coddle his students; he would exclaim at times, tongue partially in cheek, "Oh, man!" "Slave!" "Wretch!" or even "Go hang!" (in translation), in response to statements or behaviors unbefitting a Stoic.

His life was absorbed in teaching and living his philosophy. His philosophy essentially *was* his life; his life was the embodiment of his philosophy. It was a philosophy of internal mental freedom that

---

4. "When children come up to us and clap their hands and say, 'This is the good Saturnalia,' do we say to them, 'The Saturnalia are not good'? By no means, we clap our hands also." (*Discourses*, I.29.) "Who is not tempted by bright and attractive children to join in with their games, and crawl around with them, and talk baby talk with them?" (*Discourses*, II.24, in Oldfather, v. 1, 191, 417)

5. "Pancrationists."

6. "Diviners."

7. Oldfather speculates that perhaps Epictetus gestured toward his mouth and then his eye, since he does mention the eye in a later, similar passage. Still, he suggests that, perhaps inspired by the Cynic Diogenes, he pointed to another location at the back of the body!

grew in response to his years of external physical slavery. So central was his philosophy to his life that I will conclude this biographical chapter with a brief introduction to a few of the philosophical principles that defined this "lame old man," who saw his ultimate duty as "singing hymns of praise to God."

A modern scholar of Epictetus has proposed the "four unifying concepts"[8] of *freedom, judgment, volition,* and *integrity* to capture the essence and the coherence of the philosophy Epictetus expounded. I believe they bear repeating here for the light they shed on the man and his life's project.

Freedom.[9] The freedom this former slave so strongly championed was, surprisingly, not a political, economic, or social freedom, but *an inner psychological freedom that comes when one is not restrained or bound in attitude and spirit by any external thing or any internal emotional state.* We are unfree, unhappy, and unsettled when we allow things outside of our control, like other people, circumstances, events, or even illnesses, determine our internal attitudes and emotions. We are free, happy, and serene when we do only the things that we truly want to do and when we do not desire things to be other than how they truly are. This is a freedom that comes only when we have trained ourselves to want only what is truly good through an understanding of our human nature and the nature of the universe. It is a freedom that only we can give ourselves, and one that no one can take from us unless we allow them to do so.

Judgment. As we will see in chapter 5 of Epictetus's *Enchiridion,*[10] he vehemently propounded the view that people are not disturbed by things themselves but by the views they take of things. Outside of sudden, unexpected, startling shocks, such as a loud boom or a sudden painful injury, the events or circumstances that we encounter in our daily lives do not directly determine our emotions or our phys-

8. A.A. Long, *Epictetus: A Stoic and Socratic Guide to Life* (New York: Oxford University Press, 2004), 27.

9. Oldfather (v. 1, xvii) notes that freedom was so much at the forefront of Epictetus's thought that the Greek words for "free" and "freedom" appear 130 times in the extant works—six times the frequency of their occurrence in the New Testament and twice that in the works of his follower Marcus Aurelius.

10. Coincidentally, in this book's fifth chapter as well.

ical actions in response to them. We can see this in the way different individuals respond to similar hardships, losses, setbacks, illnesses, or insults. An event that devastates one person may hardly faze the next. This is because what determines our reaction to the event is not merely the event itself, but our *judgments, views, thoughts, beliefs, opinions,* or *attitudes* (to toss out some rough synonyms) in response to those events. In other words, according to Epictetus, our thoughts, what we say to ourselves about the events we encounter, are what determine our emotions and actions. When we have trained ourselves to recognize that these judgments are indeed within our control ("up to us" in another translation of *eph hemin*), we will have trained ourselves to remain undisturbed and unhindered by harmful, unhelpful, distressing emotions.

Volition. Long notes rightly that *"prohairesis"* is a favorite concept for Epictetus[11]—indeed, "the most noteworthy feature of his entire philosophy."[12] In the original Greek, *pro* means "what comes before and leads to," and *hairesis,* "choice." Aristotle used the concept, and Epictetus made his take on it central to his approach to philosophy and to life. Long translates *prohairesis* as "volition," but indicates it can be also be translated by "will." Kenneth Seddon, another modern master of Epictetus's thought, goes so far as to provide a table showing his and seventeen other English translators' ways of rendering *prohairesis.* His own preferred translation is "moral character"; others include "choice," "choices," "faculty of choice," "moral choice," "sphere of choice," "will," "freedom of choice," "moral nature," "moral personality," "volition," and "purpose."[13]

For the practical, moral purposes of this book, when summarizing Epictetus's lessons of the *Enchiridion* in our next chapter I will primarily (and hopefully quite fittingly) use *"moral purpose."* "Moral purpose" is used in the translation of W. A. Oldfather, originally published in 1928 by the Loeb Classical Library, through which

11. Scholars have tabulated a total of 168 uses of *prohaireis, prophairetic,* and *aprophairetic* in Epictetus's works.

12. Long, 28.

13. Keith Seddon, *Epictetus' Handbook and the Tablet of Cebes: Guides to Stoic Living* (New York: Routledge, 2005), 209.

I first came to know Epictetus. To my ears, the phrase is also more inspiring and ennobling than merely "volition," "will," or "purpose" unadorned with the adjective "moral." "Moral *character*" or "moral *personality*" would also be well-suited to the goals of this book, but I like the more active, dynamic, and future-looking connotations of moral *purpose*. Time and time and time again, Epictetus will exhort us to remember and live by our "moral purpose" as our highest good, our greatest gift from God.[14]

Regardless of one's choice of translation, for Epictetus, *prohairesis* is what distinguishes human beings from animals. It is what, beyond our physical bodies, makes humans what we are in terms of all of our mental faculties, abilities, thoughts, choices, character, values, goals, and self-reflective consciousness. It is what enables us to be free, to determine what is up to us and to act accordingly. It corresponds to our innermost self. To make progress in philosophy is to work toward the perfection of our *prohairesis*. It is a spark of divinity within us. *Prohairesis* is our central God-given power, but we must train ourselves to use it—our will, if you will—according to God's will. (Be ever watchful, then, for *prohairesis* in the form of "moral purpose" as we move into chapter 5.)

Integrity. Long uses the word *integrity* "to translate a cluster of terms Epictetus repeatedly uses to that can be rendered by such words as shame, reverence, trustworthiness, conscience, decency."[15] He notes that the concept of integrity is almost as central as *prohairesis,* and is not entirely separate from it. It is the way our volition is used in our relations with other people, and it "bridges the gap for Epictetus between egoism and altruism; or better, it closes the gap."[16] A person with a properly cultivated moral purpose will

14. Question 6 of the *Old Baltimore Catechism* asked, "Why did God make you?" The answer: "God made me to know him, to love him, to serve him in this world, and to be happy with Him forever in the next." Epictetus would concur with the first three clauses, though he did not share the Christian understanding of heaven. If an "*Epictetan Catechism*" were to pose the question, "What faculty did God give to us so that we might know, love, and serve Him?," Epictetus's answer would be, "God gave us the faculty of *prohairesis*."

15. Long, 30.

16. Ibid.

68

only seek goods for himself that show honor, respect, justice, benevolence, kindliness, and goodwill to others, whether or not the others reciprocate in kind. To be properly concerned with one's own welfare is to be concerned with all of the rightful social roles God has ordained that we should acquire. We'll see Epictetus's prescriptions for we might call "brotherly integrity" repeatedly and concretely in our next chapter.

Epictetus, like his beloved, stern teacher Musonius, was a man of the highest integrity. He gained the trust and respect of his students and peers because his words and his actions always matched and were always worthy of honor and emulation. Epictetus, the self-proclaimed "lame old man," died sometime around the year AD 135 at around the age of 80, but the fruits of his freedom, his judgments, his moral purpose, and his integrity can bear fruits in the lives of those living today, and likely for ages to come.

5

Lessons That Free
and Feed the Human Soul

So I am your trainer and you are being trained in my school. And my project is this—to make you unimpeded, unconstrained, unrestricted, free, contented, happy, looking to God in everything great and small. And you are here to learn and practice this.... Do you want us to begin, here and now, to execute this project? Let's say goodbye to the past. Let's simply begin, and trust me, you will see.[1]
∽ Epictetus, *Discourses* II.19, 29, 34

VERY WELL, THEN, Epictetus, let us begin to undertake your training and we will see if it builds in us those wonderful things that you claim.

In this chapter I will provide short, fast-paced summaries of the 53 chapters (most just a paragraph, and some just a sentence) of the already-summarized *Enchiridion*[2] (*Manual* or *Handbook*, if you prefer), passed down to us from Arrian. These are short, sweet, pithy epitomes or abridgements of lessons more thoroughly and leisurely addressed in the remaining four books of the original eight of the *Discourses*. Arrian composed this handbook so that readers could always have the fundamentals of Epictetus's wisdom ready at hand, so to speak, to apply in their daily life.

1. *Epictetus: A Stoic and Socratic Guide to Life*, trans. A.A. Long (New York: Oxford University Press, 2002), 123–124.

2. Also spelled *Encheiridion*, as in Oldfather.

Aided by a good half-dozen or more modern English translations in addition to the original Greek, I will endeavor to provide the gist of all 53 of them, further condensing the larger ones and striving to maintain a balance between the ancient subject matter and language of the first-century Epictetus and the needs and language of 21st-century readers. As a means of emphasizing fundamental points, an aid to their memorization, and a guide to tracking down favorite lessons within the chapters of the *Enchiridion*, I have also *italicized* key phrases and words of my choice within the summaries of each of the 53 chapters. Epictetus will mostly speak for himself in this chapter, but I would like to begin by putting readers on the look-out for these three pillars that hold up the porch of Epictetus's school. Let's simply begin, and trust me, you will see.

Three Pillars of
the Porch at Nicopolis

As we proceed through the pithy lessons of the *Handbook*, look for one of Epictetus's most unique teaching tools, his division of the practical philosophy of ethics into three fundamental concerns: (1) assent or dissent, (2) desire or aversion, and (3) choice or refusal. All three fall under the category of what is "up to us" through the rational powers of our moral purpose.

Assent or Dissent. Phantasms, that is, external impressions or appearances brought to us by our senses, are facts of the world that are beyond our control. *Reality is what it is. What lies within our power are the judgments we make about these external facts.* We have the power to seek out the truth or falsity of what we perceive, to give our *assent* to what is true and to *dissent* from and reject what is false. This requires a process of testing out the impressions and thinking through their logical consequences, since things are not always as they first appear, and we will suffer if we are misled. One's ability to test impressions will improve through ongoing training in practical reasoning when faced with real-life situations.

Desire or Aversion. In matters of assent or dissent we differentiate the *true* from the *false,* and in the related realm of desire or aversion we differentiate the *good* from the *evil.* The student in Epictetus's school learns that we court misery when we desire merely apparent goods and avoid what merely appear to be evils. *The fundamental law the student will learn is that only things within our control, within the power of our moral purpose, are truly good or evil.* Since we potentially have power over all that does fall within our moral purpose, we can develop the power to remain tranquil and joyous, even in the face of external hardships; but this will take much *askesis,* or daily training.[3]

Choice or Refusal. When we've found the true to assent to and the false to dissent from, the good to desire and the evil to avoid, we are still left with the question of what we are to do in the world, the duties we have to fulfill, the social roles that are ours to perform, the relationships with others that God has established for us so that we may help them flourish. We are called to act in accord with our moral purpose in such a way that we fulfill these responsibilities, bear with the faults of others, and share with others acts of benevolent charity.[4] *We must then train ourselves up to choose to do what is truly good and refuse to do what is evil.*

Our treatment here moved from thought to desire to choices; but I should note that according to Epictetus, actual philosophic training should begin with desire and aversion, move to choice and refusal, and then, after we attain self-mastery in these areas, focus

3. In *Discourses* II.17, Epictetus sums up the goals of the ideal student who has "become an athlete in this activity, saying, 'As for me, let everything else go; I am satisfied if I shall be free to live untrammeled and untroubled, to hold up my neck in the face of facts like a free man, and to look up to heaven as a friend of God, without fear of what may possibly happen.' Let one of you show me such a person, so that I can say to him: Enter, young man, into your own, for it is your destiny to adorn philosophy. . . ." (Oldfather, v. 1, 337).

4. In the same chapter of the second book of the *Discourses,* Epictetus says that when such a student has worked through and mastered, like an athlete, his desires and aversions, "let him then come to me and say, 'I want, it is true, to be tranquil and free from turmoil, but I want also, as a god-fearing man, a philosopher and a diligent student, to know what is my duty towards the gods, toward parents, towards brothers, towards my country, towards strangers . . . to be secure and unshaken, and not that merely in my waking hours, but also when asleep, and drunk, and melancholy mad.' Man, you are a god, great are the designs you cherish!" (Ibid.)

on improving our judgment through serious logical training.[5] These categories may sound a bit abstract thus far, and while Epictetus can get abstract and theoretical when he wants to, I think you will agree after experiencing his *Handbook* that there is hardly a figure on earth who is more practical, clear, and indeed down to earth. Let's enter his school, then, and see what our trainer has in store to whip our minds, hearts, and souls, our reason, will, and actions, into sound Stoical shape.

Pillars of Stoic Freedom

(1) *Some things are under our control, while other things are not under our control.*"[6] Epictetus starts at the very first line with the fundamental truth of Stoic psychological freedom. Some things are "*eph hemin*," "under our control," "up to us," or "within our power," as some translations have it; while other things are not. We can control things like our beliefs, choices, desires, and aversions, which are of our own doing. We cannot control things like our own bodies, possessions, reputation, or political power, which are not completely within our own power. *The key to freedom of the soul is to train oneself to know the difference between the two kinds of things.* If you treat things that are up to others as if they are up to you, you make yourself a slave to them. You'll whimper and whine, blaming both gods and men when things don't turn out as you'd like. If you always remember what you can control and what you cannot, and set your sights on what you can control, no one will be able to coerce you or hinder you; you will blame no one, accuse no one, and do nothing against your will. You will be raised above harm, because you will always recognize that those inner things that you can control cannot be taken from you. So then, if you encounter what appears to be an evil event, say to it that it is merely an impression, which you will examine according to our

---

5. Twelve centuries later St. Thomas Aquinas would give similar advice for those seeking spiritual perfection. It is when one has mastered the moral virtues of temperance, fortitude, prudence, and justice that one is best prepared for the contemplation of the truths of God.
6. Oldfather, v. 2, 483 (italics added).

rule. If it concerns something that is not under your control, tell it that it is nothing to you!

(2) As for *desires* and *aversions*, when you fail to get what you desire, that is *un*fortunate; and when some bad thing happens that you hoped to avoid, that is a case of *mis*fortune. You will avoid misfortune if you are only averse to things that are within your control and that are contrary to nature. But if you are averse to illness and death and other things beyond our control, you will eventually meet misfortune. For those starting in philosophy, don't even think about desires at first; you will end up unfortunate since you have not trained yourself yet in how to desire and acquire what is truly good.

(3) Next, Epictetus gives the advice that we quoted and heeded in this book's introduction, that we remember to ask of everything we find attractive or useful, or of which we are fond, "*What is your nature?*" And here in his simple, earthy brilliance, Epictetus starts with the example of a mere pot or a jug. If you say to yourself, "I am fond of a jug!," you will not be disappointed when it breaks, since you will remember that fragility is part of its nature. So far, so easy. Now, consider too the nature of your child or your wife, and when you kiss them remind yourself that you kiss a fragile, mortal human being, so that if they should die, you will not be devastated.

(4) *Every one of our daily undertakings provides opportunity to practice the principle of freeing the soul by recognizing what is within our control and what isn't.* You are heading out to the public baths today? Remind yourself that people are going to splash you, jostle you, and maybe even insult you or steal your clothing. Say to yourself from the start that you want to take a bath, but you also want to keep your choices, indeed your very moral purpose, in accord with reason and nature. Then, if you are splashed, jostled, insulted, or robbed, you will remind yourself that you wanted to bathe, but you also wanted to act in harmony with nature; and therefore you will choose not to be annoyed at those less important things beyond your control.[7]

---

7. Perhaps a worthwhile practice for every time we buckle up and take our cars out on the road!

The Porch and the Cross

(5) *"What upsets people is not things themselves, but their judgments about the things."*[8] Here Epictetus unveils another key pillar, a pillar which would go on to become the acknowledged cornerstone of 20th-century cognitive psychotherapy.[9] This passage is often also rendered as follows: *"People are disturbed not by things, but by the views they take of things."* This implies that by changing the ways we look at things we can *choose not to upset ourselves.* Here Epictetus starts with no simple jug or pot but with that which humans fear most, death itself. Death itself is not fearful, he says, or otherwise the wise Socrates would have faced it with dread rather than calmly. Whenever we let the fear of death, let alone a myriad of other lesser events, distress us, we have only ourselves to blame. Epictetus concludes with a pithy lesson well worth pondering, memorizing, and applying. People uneducated in Stoic philosophy blame *others* when things go wrong; those who have begun such an education blame *themselves*; those whose education is complete blame *no one* at all.

(6) Epictetus tells us not to be elated with joy over any excellence that is not our own. If a horse itself were to exclaim with joy, "Look at me, I'm beautiful!," we could put up with that; but if you are inclined to brag joyfully about your beautiful horse, bear in mind you are joyful not about *your own* good, but about the good of the horse.[10] *Why not then be joyful about that which is truly your own—your ability to choose how you will deal with impressions or*

8. *Epictetus: The Handbook,* trans. Nicholas P. White (Indianapolis: Hackett Publishing Co., 1983), 13 (italics added).

9. That story will be told in our next legacy chapter.

10. Catholic theologian St. Frances de Sales was no stranger to Epictetan wisdom. In counseling against the sin of vainglory he writes: "Vainglory is the glory that we give ourselves; either for what is not really in us, or for what is in fact in us but not owing to anything we did, or for what is in us and owing to us but which does not deserve to be the cause of a boast.... There are those who are proud and haughty because they ride a magnificent horse or because their hat sports a fancy feather, or because they are wearing some fashionable clothing. Who does not see the folly here? If there is glory due, it belongs to the horse, the bird or the tailor! And what a pitiable heart is his who expects esteem because of a horse, a feather or some lace!" *Introduction to the Devout Life: A Popular Abridgment,* ed. Madame Yvonne Stephan (Rockford, IL: TAN Books, 1990), part III, ch. 5, 126.

appearances? If you do so in harmony with nature, enjoy away, for your joy is truly joy for a good of your own!

(7) Next Epictetus takes us on a sea voyage and has us imagine that our boat has anchored. Go ahead, he says, and snatch up some fresh water and a shellfish and vegetable while you are at it, but always stay mindful of the boat so that you'll *be ready when the Captain calls.* If he calls you must be ready to drop those other things, if need be, to get back to the boat on time. Life is such a voyage. If you are blessed with a wife and a child instead of a vegetable and a shellfish, they are no hindrance to you; but if the Captain calls, you cannot take those things with you. You must be prepared to leave them behind. Indeed, if you are very old, never go far from the boat, so you won't be left behind or be hauled away kicking and screaming.

(8) Here is paragraph 8, in its entirety: "*Do not seek to have everything that happens happen as you wish, but wish for everything to happen as it actually does happen, and your life will be serene.*"[11]

(9) Disease harms our bodies, but not our moral purpose, unless we let it. Lameness impedes our leg, not our moral purpose. So say this to each event that happens to you and you will find that it interferes with something else, not with *you.*

(10) *Whenever something happens to you, says Epictetus, remember to ask yourself what capacities you have for dealing with it.* If you see a beautiful body, call forth your *self-control.* If hardship comes your way, get out your *endurance.* If you are insulted, find your *patience.* If you *train yourself in this every day,* appearances will not carry you away.

From Devastation to Invincibility

(11) Whenever something or someone you had is gone, don't say, "I lost it," but rather say, "*I have given it back.*" If your wife or your child dies, then they were given back. If your farm is taken, it too was given back. If it was taken by a scoundrel, it is not your con-

11. Oldfather, v. 2, 490.

cern how the Giver asked for it back. Treat whatever you are given as something not your own, like travelers while staying at an inn.

(12) *There is a price to pay for tranquility.* If you want to make progress in wisdom, give up all worries that if you neglect your business you'll have nothing to live on, or that if you don't punish your slave boy he'll turn out bad. It's better to die of hunger without distress than to live in plenty with a troubled mind. So too is it better that your slave boy be bad than that you make yourself unhappy over it. Start with the small things. If your oil or wine gets stolen, tell yourself this is simply the price of tranquility, the price of not being upset. Nothing comes for free. When you call to your slave boy, it's up to him whether he pays attention or chooses to do what you ask, but it is not up to him whether or not you are disturbed.

(13) *If you want to make progress in wisdom, let people think you are a hopeless fool when it comes to the kind of external things they care about.* If you acquire a reputation for being learned in non-essential things, take a hard look at yourself. It is no easy thing to focus both on your moral purpose and external things, and a person who devotes his attention to one of these things will end up neglecting the other.

(14) How foolish you are if you desire that your children and your wife live forever, since you are treating things outside of your control as if they were inside it, and things that are not yours as if they were. *You are capable, however, of not failing to get what you desire, if you desire only what is within your power.* A master has the power to give or take away what a slave desires. *If you would be free, don't desire things within another's power or you'll render yourself a slave.*

(15) *Remember that life is like a banquet and you should always act accordingly.* If something is passed to you, reach out and take a reasonable portion. If the plate passes by you, don't hold it back. If it hasn't made it to you yet, don't stretch out your arm and go reaching for it. Mind your manners! Don't stretch out your desires. Be patient and wait. Behave the same way toward your wife and family, toward your job, and toward wealth, and you will render yourself worthy to share a banquet with the gods. If you should come to despise even delicacies when they are set before

you, you will not only dine with the gods, but even rule with them. This is how people like Diogenes and Heraclitus acted and why they were rightly called gods.[12]

(16) When you see someone wailing in grief because their child has gone away or they have lost their property, don't get carried away by the impression that the external situation is bad; but be ready to say to yourself that what saddens him is not merely the situation itself (since others would not be crushed in similar circumstances), but his judgment about it. By all means, show him sympathy, and groan along with him if need be, but *do not moan on the inside.*

(17) *Remember that you are an actor in a play that is determined by the Playwright.* He determines if it's short or long. Whether he wants you to play a beggar, a lame man, a ruler or a private citizen, *what is up to you is to play your assigned part well.*

(18) When a crow croaks in an ominous way, don't let the impression carry you away with fear, but tell yourself that ominous signs do not affect you but only perhaps your paltry body or your petty possessions, reputation, children, or wife. For *all signs are good signs if you wish, since it is up to you to find benefit from whatever life should bring.*

(19) *If you would be invincible, enter no contest that you cannot win.* (You can't lose if you don't play, we might say!) Make sure you only play the game that really counts. Don't think someone who has gained honor, power, or a good reputation is necessarily rendered happy. If what is truly of value is what is truly up to you, there is no room for envy or jealousy. You will not desire to become a general, a legislator, or a leader, but you'll desire to be free. *To become free you must not set your sights on things outside your control.*

(20) *Remember that insults don't harm you; only the judgment you make that they are insulting does.* Note well that when someone bothers you, it is really your own belief that produces your dis-

12. Diogenes the Cynic and Heraclitus the pre-Socratic philosopher (see the introduction), who along with Socrates and Zeno were considered Stoic sages, god-like in their indifference to things outside their control.

comfort. So then, don't get carried away by appearances and act too swiftly when insulted or annoyed. If you pause to cool down and reflect on the realities beneath the appearances, you will regain your self-control and composure.

From Death to Duties

(21) *Don't try to avoid thinking about things that appear terrible, like death or illness, but look at them squarely every day and you will not be carried away by contemptible thoughts or petty desires.*

(22) *If you love philosophy, brace yourself for ridicule and abuse* from those who will call out, "Here comes the philosopher! Look at his nose in the air!" But don't reject philosophy, and don't put on airs either. Stick to your worthy aspirations as if you were assigned to them by God. If you stick to your principles, those who laugh will later admire you; but if you cave in, then you'll be laughed at twice over.

(23) In the same vein, if you abandon your principles in hopes of pleasing others, you have lowered your standards and lost your way. *Be content, then, to be a philosopher whether you thereby please others or not.* And if you would be a philosopher, appear one to yourself, and you will become capable of living a life in pursuit of wisdom.

(24) Don't fear that you will receive no honors and be a nobody if you don't obtain some high public position or get invited to fancy parties. You think lack of honors a bad thing? How can *you* be in a bad or shameful state because of the actions of *others?* You worry that you won't be able to help your friend if you don't gain an office or accrue great wealth? Perhaps your friends even encourage you to do so that they might become citizens or get some cash from you. If you can do it in an honorable way while maintaining self-respect, perhaps you will choose to do so; but such wishes of theirs are not up to you. Your friends will be better off with an honest, trustworthy friend than with a friend who has forsaken his dignity for wealth or for office. *Strive to be a good citizen in as humble a position as may befit you and you will serve yourself, your friends, and your city best.*

(25) And as for yet more on honor, *if someone else has been given a greater honor than you, a higher place at the table, or perhaps they, and not you, have been sought out for advice, ask yourself if the honors are good or bad. If they are bad, then you don't need them. If they are good, you should be glad that the other has received them.* Further, have such honors truly been your goals? If they were won at the price of flattery or servitude, are you willing to pay this price at such cost to your moral purpose?

(26) *How easy to give advice after loss and how hard to put ourselves in other people's shoes.* Your friend's slave boy breaks his mug and you tell him, "It's just one of those things, shrug it off!" How do you act when *your* mug is broken? Take this small lesson and apply it to big things. When a friend's wife or child dies, do you say, "Such is life"; and yet when yours does do you wail out "Woe is me!"? *Remember then how you feel when you hear of such things that have happened to others.*

(27) *Just as a target is not set up in order to be missed, neither are things that exist in nature bad or evil in themselves.*[13]

(28) Think how angry you would be if someone turned over your *body* to any person who happened to cross your path. Well, then, why are you not ashamed to your turn over your *mind* to any person who happens along, so that when he insults or slights you, you allow your thoughts to become disturbed and upset?

(29) *If you set your sights on some goal, think out in advance the long sequence of behaviors that must lead up to it and follow it.* You would wear the glorious laurel wreath of the Olympic athlete? It's a fine thing indeed; but are you willing to eat a strict diet, train relentlessly, forgo wine, turn yourself over to the orders of a trainer, and be willing to dislocate your shoulder, sprain your ankle, wrench your spine, eat a mouthful of dirt, and after all that suffer defeat? Think about such things, and then go for it if you still want it. Otherwise you'll become like the child who will be a gladiator one day, a trumpeter then next, and an actor the day after that, or indeed like a monkey who does what he sees. Be a

---

13. Epictetus, like his teacher Musonius Rufus, concurs with the lesson of Genesis 1 that all that God has made is good.

philosopher, not a dilettante. Find the pursuits that are truly fitting for you and then pursue them if you are willing to pay the
price. *Ultimately, your heart must be set either on externals or on
your ruling principle. It's up to you whether you choose the role of a
philosopher or that of a non-philosopher.*

(30) *We find our true duties by examining our social relationships.*
You have a father? Then take care of him. "But he is not a good
father." Did nature determine that you would have a *good* father?
No, only that you would have a father. "My brother has harmed
me." Well, then, maintain your brotherly relation with him. Focus
not on what he has done, but on how you can keep the responses
you choose in harmony with nature. *Another person can't truly
harm you unless you allow it. You are harmed when you choose to
think you have been harmed.* So then, keep this in mind, indeed,
make it a habit, as you consider what duties to expect from your
neighbor, fellow citizen, or commanding officer.

On Building One's Character: From Piety to Modesty

(31) We best show piety to the gods when we hold true *beliefs*
about them—that they exist and administer the universe justly—
and when we submit our *wills* to their judgment, accepting that
the universe is as it is for a purpose and whatever happens does so
for a purpose. In this way, you will not blame the gods or accuse
them of negligence. *To achieve such piety, we must detach our ideas
of what is good and what is bad from what is not up to us, and focus
our thoughts every day on the things that are up to us.* Otherwise, we
will blame the gods, when we focus only on externals that seem
evil and purposeless at the surface level rather than in the light of
the grander scheme. We cannot have pious feelings toward the
gods if we erroneously believe they are causing us harm. When we
properly tend to our desires and aversions in accordance with reason and nature, we show piety to the gods. Further, it is always
appropriate to make libations[14] and sacrifices and to give the gods

---

14. A portion of a drink, most often wine, that pious Greeks would pour out in
offering to the gods before they drank the rest. (Some ancient sources tell of some
stingy, rather less-than-pious people had who mastered the art of a quick flick of
the wrist that would spill merely a drop.)

first-fruits according to the traditions of our fathers, and to do so with pure hearts and with liberal generosity.

(32) Would you go to a fortune-teller? Bear in mind that even if their predictions are right, they have nothing of value to tell you. *You have no need of a fortune-teller to tell you to always do what is right and just, regardless of what the outcome might be.* Remember how that most great diviner, Pythian Apollo, threw out of his temple a man who did not help his friend when he was being murdered.[15]

(33) *Decide what kind of a character you will build, and maintain it whether you are alone or with others.* Be silent when you can. Listen more than you speak. Stick to your bare needs for bodily things like clothing, food, drink, housing and possessions. Get rid of anything you hold just for the sake of reputation or luxury. As for sex, stay pure before marriage, but don't be angry with those who do not abstain, and don't boast about your abstinence. If someone tells you that somebody else is saying bad things about you, don't defend yourself, but merely say, "That person obviously did not know about all of my other faults, or he would have brought those up too." When you have to go to public events, don't get carried away by the mob, but maintain your honor and dignity. *When you are about to meet someone of prominence, ask yourself, "What would Socrates or Zeno have done in this situation?"* Expect to be shunned or ignored if you desire or need to call on a person of importance, and do not be distressed if you are told he isn't home or if he pays you no attention. In conversation, don't carry on about your own deeds and accomplishments. It is not as pleasant for others to hear what has happened to you as it is for you to talk about it. And avoid becoming a buffoon or slipping into vulgarity. When another person uses foul language in your presence, tell him you do not appreciate it, if the opportunity arises; and if not, you can get your message across by your silence or your frown at his words.

(34) *Be on your guard when faced with apparent pleasures. Don't be carried away by first appearances, but wait for a while and give your-*

---

15. The story refers to the god Apollo at the Oracle of Delphi and the idea that one should not need a fortune-teller to know that one should defend one's country or one's friend in spite of possible harm to oneself.

self time to think. Then call to mind two times, not only the time in which you'll enjoy that pleasure, but the time afterwards when you'll berate yourself for your action. Then imagine instead how you will be truly pleased and worthy of self-praise if you refrain from it. If there are times when it is reasonable to indulge in a particular pleasant action, even then don't get carried away by its charm, pleasure, and attractiveness, but also keep in mind how much better it is to win victory over your desires for pleasure.

(35) *If you determine that it is right to do some action, then never try to hide it, even if others might misinterpret it and think you are up to no good. If it is not the right thing to do, then don't do it.* But if it is, why should you be afraid of those who criticize you wrongly?

(36) *Think of your actions in their complete context and moderate them accordingly.* When you have a meal with others, remember not only the pleasure and nourishment that would come from grabbing an overly large portion, but also the respectful behavior you owe to your host.

(37) *If you take on some position or project beyond your true capacity, you will bring disgrace on yourself;* and by taking on an inappropriate role, you will be neglecting to take on a role that truly is fitting for you.

(38) *Just as when walking you are careful not to step on a nail or twist your ankle, take care not to bring harm to your ruling principle.*[16] If we exercise such care with every action, we will act more securely.

(39) *Regarding your possessions, the body provides the true measure of your needs, as the nature of the foot calls for the need for shoes. To get carried away beyond true need is to walk over a cliff.* Even with shoes, if you go beyond the measure of the needs of the foot, you will think you need gilded shoes and then shoes with purple embroidery. The sky is the limit once a thing moves beyond its true measure.

16. In Stoic psychology, the *hegemonikon* is the essential part of the soul that can discern the good and choose to act upon it. Various translations use "ruling principle," "governing principle," "ruling faculty," or simply "mind."

(40) Females are called "ladies" or "mistresses" right after they turn fourteen. If they see they are valued as nothing but bedmates for men, they place all their focus on their appearance and place all their hopes on luring a man. *We should rather take care to make clear to young women that they are valued not only for their attractiveness, but for appearing modest and showing self-respect in their dress and manner.*

Tending the Temple of the Body and Mind

(41) *It is the mark of a small mind to be excessively focused on the concerns of the body,* with excessive exercising, eating, drinking, and sexual activity. You must keep these things in their proper place, doing them in passing, but focus your attention fully on the ruling part of your soul.

(42) *If someone insults you or treats you badly, remember that he believes it is right for him to do so.* He acts according to *his* perspective and not according to *yours.* If he interprets your words or actions wrongly, it is he who is harmed and deceived. *If you keep this principle in mind, you will be gentle with those who abuse you, saying to yourself every time, "It seemed that way to him."*

(43) *Everything has two handles, and only one of them is suitable for carrying.* If your brother harms you, don't grab hold of the handle that he treated you unjustly, but instead grab the handle that he is the brother who was raised with you. In this way you will grasp the handle that is suitable to carry this situation.

(44) These are invalid statements: "I'm richer than you; therefore I am better than you," and "I'm more eloquent than you; therefore I'm better than you." Here are their valid forms: "I'm richer than you; therefore my property is greater than yours," and "I'm more eloquent than you; therefore my manner of speaking is superior to yours." *You are neither your possessions nor your speech.*

(45) Does a man bathe too quickly? Don't say he bathes badly, but that he bathes quickly. Does someone drink a great deal of wine? Don't say he is a wino, but that he drinks a great deal of wine. *You do not know the other person's reasons for their actions, so how can*

*you know from outward appearances whether their actions were
done badly?*

(46) *Would you be a philosopher? Then never call yourself one, and
don't talk a great deal about it among non-philosophers, but rather
show your philosophy through your actions.* Don't give a discourse
on proper eating at a banquet; eat properly at a banquet. Remember how Socrates was so free of ostentation and self-importance
that when people came to him asking him to introduce them to
other philosophers, he would take them.[17] Socrates did not mind
being overlooked, so why should we? Also, if philosophical talk
crops up in the conversations of non-philosophers, be hesitant to
put your two-cents' worth in, spewing out what you have not yet
fully digested. When someone says you don't know anything and it
doesn't bother you, then you will know you are making a good
start in philosophy. Sheep don't show how well they have eaten by
vomiting up their grass before their shepherd, but by digesting
their food and producing wool and milk. So too for you, *don't
regurgitate philosophical propositions to non-philosophers, but show
them the actions such propositions lead to in one's life, once they are
digested.*

(47) *When you have trained yourself to live simply according to
bodily needs, don't boast and show off about it.* If you drink only
water, then drink it, but don't look for every opportunity to tell
people you drink only water. Discipline yourself for yourself and
not for outward show. *Don't go around hugging statues!*[18] *Instead,
if you are very thirsty, take some cold water into your mouth and spit
it out when no one is looking.*

(48) *The condition and character of those uneducated in philosophy:*

---

17. This calls to mind a similar event in the life of St. Thomas Aquinas. A religious brother visiting the Dominican convent at Paris chanced upon Thomas upon
arriving and ordered Thomas to guide him around the city, chiding him at times
for walking too slowly. The brother was later aghast when he learned that the man
who so humbly submitted to his commands and withstood his rebukes was the
world's most renowned philosopher and theologian.

18. This is an illusion to the Cynic Diogenes, who reportedly would train himself in toughness, and make a show of it, by hugging cold statues displayed outdoors in public places in the midst of winter.

• Never to look for good or harm to come from themselves, but to expect them to come from others.

The condition and character of those educated in philosophy:

• Always to look for good or bad to come from within oneself.

Signs of progress in philosophy:

• To blame or praise no one.
• Never to talk about oneself as accomplished or learned.
• When faced with failure, to look to oneself for the reasons.
• When praised by another, to smile to oneself and take it lightly.
• To move through life carefully like an invalid whose limbs are healing and are not yet strong.
• To eliminate selfish desires and to only seek to avoid things—contrary to nature.
• To diminish impulsive behavior.
• To care not if others consider you foolish or ignorant.

In a word, the person progressing in philosophy watches himself as if he were an enemy lying in wait.

(49) Don't put on airs if you can explain the great works of a philosopher like Chrysippus,[19] but say to yourself that if Chrysippus had written more clearly himself, you would have nothing to boast about. What should we want? To understand nature and to live our lives in harmony with it. If we hear that Chrysippus knew how to understand nature and live by it but we can't understand him, then we seek out someone who can explain his writings to us. Now, when we do find someone who can explain him, we must live according to the things he has explained. If we are moved only by the excellence of the explanation, then we have become grammarians, not philosophers. *No, our task is not to read or explain Chrysippus, but to live our lives in harmony with the wisdom in his lessons.*

(50) *When presented with valid principles, treat them as if they were the law and it would be sacrilegious to go against them. Pay no*

19. Chrysippus of Soli (279–206 BC), one of the most influential and prolific of the Greek Stoics.

attention if others speak poorly about you, since their words are not within your control.

The Time to Begin is *Now,* by Zeus!

(51) *How* long are you going to consider yourself unworthy of pursuing the best things and never going against the conclusions of reason? You have learned the right philosophic principles and agreed with them, so when are you going to put them into action? You are not a boy anymore, but a full-grown man. If you procrastinate and make excuses for focusing day after day on non-essential things, you will live on in ignorance until the day you die. So, be a man (or a woman)! *Declare to yourself today that you will always act according to what is right and best. If you find it hard, buck up! The contest is now; you are in the Olympic games of life today, and you cannot put things off anymore, delaying your progress for even one more day.* Socrates became perfect by paying attention to nothing but his reason in every life situation. *Even if you are not yet another Socrates, get out there and live like you want to become one!*

(52) In terms of the discipline of philosophy itself, the first important project is finding out whether certain statements about things are true or false. The second project is that of logical demonstrations; for example, of why one should not adhere to what is false. The third project is the confirmation and explanation of the second; such as analyzing why some proof is a proof, or even what is a proof, and what are truth and falsity. Therefore, the first project gives rise to the need for the second and the second to the third. They follow logically. The most important, however, is the *first* project; and yet too often we focus merely on the third, neglecting the first altogether.[20] Therefore, *we believe false things and act upon false beliefs, yet we stand quite ready to prove to someone that he should not believe what is false.*

---

20. Perhaps many modern university students exposed to philosophy courses would conclude that Epictetus was quite prescient in describing the course of much of modern academic philosophy, with such a focus on words about words, and so little emphasis on what things are truly true or false, right or wrong, for those who would live good and thoughtful lives, informed by their pursuit of wisdom.

(53) On a parting note, *memorize* the gist of these great thoughts and *stand ready to use them every day of your life:*

Lead me thou on, O Zeus, and Destiny,
To that whatever goal you assign me.
I will follow and not falter,
But even if my will proves weak and craven,
I'll follow anyway.
Whoever has rightly complied with necessity
Is counted wise and skilled in things divine.
Well, O Crito, if it is pleasing to the gods, then let it be so.
Anytus and Meletus can kill me, but they cannot harm me.[21]

From Lessons to Legacy

Arrian compiled the condensed *Handbook* of Epictetus's wisdom not as a book to be read once and forgotten, but as a book to be read again and again, digested, and re-digested, lived and re-lived with benefit throughout the course of one's life. Hopefully, the reader will have found some ideas worth chewing on and will be motivated to seek out more, both in the appetizing *Handbook* and in the full four-course banquet spread out in the *Discourses*. Next we will survey what the world has made of Epictetus's thought, from his contemporary philosophers and theologians, to later world leaders and literary figures, and right up to modern psychologists, social workers, novelists, and even jet-fighter pilots.

---

21. The first of these lines is from Cleanthes's (331–232 BC) *Hymn to Zeus*. He followed Zeno and preceded Chrysippus as head of the Stoic school at Athens. The second lines are from a fragment 965 of the Greek tragedian Euripides (480–406 BC). The third line is based upon Plato's *Crito* (43d), and the last upon Plato's *Apology* (30c–d), both of which are presented as quotations from Socrates. (My translations, after consulting several modern English translations and the original Greek in Oldfather.)

6

A Legacy of Integrity
Integral to Mental Well-Being

It is easy, indeed, to observe that Plato is found only in the hands of those who profess to be literary men; while Epictetus is admired by persons of ordinary capacity, who have a desire to be benefited, and who perceive the improvement which may be derived from his writings. ∼ Origen, *Contra Celsus* VI.2

Slave, poor as Irus, halting as I trod,
I, Epictetus, was the friend of God.[1]

✝

AFTER EPICTETUS'S DEATH around the year AD 135, during the reign of Emperor Hadrian, his philosophy lived on most vigorously in the writings of the successor of Hadrian's successor, the Emperor Marcus Aurelius. Part IV of this book will tell the story of how the Stoic slave inspired the Stoic Emperor, the man sometimes called "The Last Stoic." In this chapter, we will highlight Epictetus's vast and continuing legacy beyond the Stoic porch and into our own land and time, as we examine his influence upon early Christian Church Fathers, writers of monastic rules, medieval philosophers, German emperors, Renaissance philosophers, American presidents and literary giants, founders of systems of cognitive psychotherapy, modern novelists, fighter pilots, vice-presidential candidates, and present-day men and women from all walks of life and all faiths.

---

1. Ibid., vii. (An anonymous epigram found in the writings of St. John Chrysostom and Macrobius.)

The Porch and the Cross

The third-century Church Father Origen, you might recall from chapter 3, sang the praises of Musonius Rufus as a "model of excellence of life." Our quotation above shows that he also thought highly of Rufus's star Stoic student. Origen brings the writings of Epictetus into his response to those who hold that the relatively plain and homely writings of the Scriptures are inferior to the elegant writings of the Greek philosophers like Plato. He uses the works of Epictetus as an example of the kind of plain, ethical writings that appeal to all people and not merely literary connoisseurs. And no doubt Epictetus himself would approve. Recall Arrian's claim that Epictetus cared little for flowery words and elegant presentation, but uttered his words "clearly aiming at nothing else but to incite the minds of his hearers to the best of things." The works of Epictetus, like the Holy Scriptures, are accessible and aimed at the spiritual betterment of all, not merely the amusement of the elite.

Our second quotation is said to be an anonymous epigram that appears in the writings of the fifth-century Roman Macrobius, and also those of the fourth-century (AD 349–407) Father and Doctor of the Church, and Archbishop of Constantinople, St. John Chrysostom. Here we see not only his plain style and wholesome ethical advice, but also the perception that Epictetus was a "friend of God" highlighted in the work of a prominent Greek-speaking and -writing Christian theologian. So what else drew early Christians to the wisdom of Epictetus? Let's take a quick look at this early legacy.

The God of the Philosophers and of Epictetus

Different Stoics had different conceptions of God. The Stoics were no atheists. Though there were, of course, no Darwinian "new atheists" at the time of their philosophical heyday as there are in our day, there were indeed materialistic atheists of other schools, such as the Atomists, most notably Democritus and Leucippus, who saw all of reality as composed of atoms moving about according to chance, leaving no room for the soul or for spiritual beings. Other contemporary philosophers, like the Epicureans, most notably Epicurus himself and Lucretius, drew from the Atomists; and, while still believing in gods, they paved the way for later atheism by arguing that the gods were uninterested and unable to intervene in our affairs. They also denied an afterlife, and saw the highest good as pleasure rather than conforming one's will to God's.

The Stoics did not deny the gods, and some saw the reality of a single God. Aided by reason but lacking in divine revelation, they had varied conceptions of God that captured pieces and parts of the truths of His nature.

God was considered a spiritual and active principle that gives shape and meaning to a primary passive principle of undifferentiated matter. The ancient Greeks, you see, had a conception of an eternal universe (an existence that always existed) and perceived God as a First Cause in terms of *changing* and *forming* matter rather than bringing the universe into existence *ex nihilo*—that is, out of nothing. The Stoics had rather vague and sometimes conflicting understandings of God as the shaper of the cosmos, or universe; as the "soul" of the universe; or as the universe itself. Some held, therefore, a rather pantheistic view that everything is God, or a part of God. Some saw Him as synonymous with Nature or with Fate. Others, most especially Epictetus, did see God as a personal, father-like figure interested in our existence.

Epictetus believed, as did early Christian Church Fathers, that human reason leads to the undeniable existence of God. Scripture relates that "from the greatness and beauty of created things comes a corresponding perception of their Creator" (Wis. 13:5).[2] Further, St. Paul relates that "ever since the creation of the world his [God's] invisible nature, namely, his eternal power and deity, has been clearly perceived in the things that have been made" (Rom. 1:20). Starting with the evidence of our senses and reasoning back from effects we can see to their causes, their cause's causes, and finally to an unavoidable First Cause: we are led to the inevitability of a God who sustains and orders all that exists. This would eventually be declared a dogma of the Catholic Church at the First Vatican Council in 1870: "If anyone says that the one, true God, our creator and

---

2. *The Holy Bible containing the Old and New Testaments*, Revised Standard Version, Catholic Edition (San Francisco: Ignatius Press, 1966).

lord, cannot be known with certainty from the things that have been made, by the natural light of human reason: let him be anathema."

Epictetus's natural reason did lead him to God, whom he sometimes call God and sometimes Zeus, the chief of the Greek Gods whose name essentially means God—*Theos,* or, in Latin, *Deus,* as in deity. In *Discourses* II.15, Epictetus gives this parable of men attending a fair:

> "What then is the universe," they ask, "and who governs it? No one? Yet how can it be that, while it is impossible for a city or a household to remain even a very short time without someone to govern and care for it, nevertheless this great and beautiful structure should be kept in such orderly arrangement by sheer accident and chance? There must be, therefore, One who governs it."[3]

Here Epictetus foreshadows, in some measure, Aquinas's "fifth way" to demonstrate the existence of God based on based on "the governance of the world."[4] Epictetus then presents essential follow-up questions we must address once we acknowledge that God exists:

> "What kind of being is He, and how does he govern it (the universe)? And what are we, who have been created by Him, and for what purpose were we created? Do we, then, really have some contact and relation with Him or none at all?"[5]

Let's quickly run down some of Epictetus's own answers to those questions he posed. Here and there in the *Handbook* and again and again in the *Discourses*, in different contexts and from different

---

3. Oldfather, v. 1, 307.

4. "Ex gubernatione rerum" in Aquinas's Latin (*Summa Theologica* I, Q. 2.a.3.). In a manner that might satisfy Epictetus himself, and largely due to the influence of Aristotle, Aquinas believed that reason alone could not settle the issue of whether the universe always existed with God or was created in time. He therefore crafted the "five ways" to show that even if the universe was not *created* in time, or was co-existent with God, it could not be *sustained* in existence without God's causal power. None of his arguments depend on a backward progression of causes into time, but on the need for God's causal power *at this very moment.*

5. Oldfather, v. 1, 307. (Note well the similarity to the crucial question from the *Baltimore Catechism* cited in our chapter 5!)

angles, Epictetus asserts that God is an all-wise and all-seeing being who governs the universe justly. We are made in his image, with a spark of his divine spirit in the form of our rational nature, unique among all creatures on earth. As for our relationship to God, he is our Father; we are akin to Him, and to all our fellow human beings. We were made to sing him hymns of praise and to honor him by acting in accordance with our God-given moral purpose, assenting only to truth, desiring only the good, and choosing only actions that benefit the universal brotherhood of mankind. Those who have the vocation to become philosophers have been chosen by Him to serve as His messengers, to deliver the news, through their words and through their manner of life, to all people about how to be saved by living in harmony with His will.

In Epictetus's philosophy, knowledge of abstract theories and mastery of the intricacies of logic are not unimportant; but neither are they central. Recall that mastery of assent and dissent is the third and final stage for the student of philosophy. What matters most to Epictetus is to live a good life in accordance with nature or the universal law. As for God's primary role in achieving this goal, Epictetus states:

> Now the philosophers say that the first thing we must learn is this: That there is a God, and that He provides for the universe, and that it is impossible for a man to conceal from Him, not merely his actions, but even his purposes and his thoughts.[6]

Epictetus goes on to say that we must then learn what God is like and try to please Him by resembling Him in things like faithfulness, freedom, beneficence, and high-mindedness. In sum, "therefore, in everything he [the person who would please God] says and does, he must act as an imitator of God."[7]

When we add to such passages Epictetus's use of the same Greek words and phrases found in the New Testament that we translate into such words and phrases as "vocation," "salvation," "to convert," "Lord, have mercy on us," "thank God," and "knowledge of the

6. Ibid., 301.
7. Ibid.

95

truth,"[8] it is no surprise that early Christians perceived an affinity (and perhaps a shared "spark of divinity") within the works of the Stoic Epictetus.

As for Epictetus's actual knowledge of and contact with Christian thought, he refers to Christianity or Christians apparently only twice in his surviving work. In *Discourses* II.9, he refers to those who claim to be "Jews" (possibly meaning "Christians"), who are "counterfeit baptists" in that they proclaim their faith but do not live it out in their lives. He implies that to confess the Christian faith and to live it is a rare and rigorous undertaking, mastered by only a few. He urges his students not to be like the "counterfeit baptists" by failing to practice the rational principles they preach. In *Discourses* IV.7, he describes the "Galileans" as people who can overcome the fear of tyrants through their *faith* in God. He urges his students to use their *reason* to grasp God's providence and likewise relinquish their fears.

Epictetus provides yet more fodder for Christian thought. Throughout his remaining works he inculcates a morality in keeping with the last seven of the Ten Commandments, pertaining to man's relations with man. He strongly exhorts us to honor our parents and to abstain from killing or harming others; goes on at great length about how the adulterer gives up all about him that is honorable and noble; encourages us to seek and speak only the truth; and to become free of covetousness for things outside our control, including our neighbor's wife. As for the first three commandments, relating to God, he constantly encourages us to honor God above all else. Though I can't recall a passage where he talks about using God's name in vain, he writes again and again that we should never blame God or slip into vulgarity. Though he did not speak specifically of a Sabbath or Lord's Day, he exhorts us to keep Cleanthes's prayer to Zeus in our thoughts every day of our lives.

Though they appear nowhere in a single list in Epictetus's writings (and they don't in the Bible, either), the Eastern and Western Christian traditions that produced what started as "eight assailing

8. For the original Greek words and a fuller treatment of this point, see K. Ierodiakonou, *The Philosopher as God's Messenger*, in A. Mason & T. Scaltas, eds., *The Philosophy of Epictetus* (New York: Oxford University Press, 2007).

thoughts" of Evagrius of Pontus (345–399) and culminated in Pope St. Gregory the Great's (540–604) list of "seven deadly sins" can all be found at some point, and are condemned soundly, within the surviving works of Epictetus, as he advises his students against gluttony, lust, vainglory, envy, avarice, and slothful negligence of the things that matter most.

Though he did not focus on the cardinal virtues of prudence, justice, temperance, and courage as his teacher Musonius Rufus did, let alone develop and expand the list further as we will see in the writings of Seneca, these virtues are mentioned from time to time in his writings. His main moral focus was on a trained moral purpose *(prohairesis)*, for him the font from which all virtues flow and all vices are washed away.

God's Lame Messenger in Plato's Academy?

A testimony to Epictetus's profound historical influence after the demise of Stoicism and outside the realm of Christian thought can be seen in the treatment of Epictetus's *Handbook* provided in a massive *Commentary* written by Simplicius of Cilia (ca. AD 490–560). Simplicius was not a Stoic, but a Neoplatonist, a follower of Plato, who was known for his commentaries on many of Aristotle's works. Nevertheless, for instructing beginning students of philosophy in the foundations of ethical living, his choice was none other than Epictetus's *Handbook*. The *Handbook* itself takes up about 20 to 30 pages in a modern book. Simplicius's *On Epictetus' Handbook* is more than 10 times as long! He found the book an excellent source of practical wisdom, and he also used it as a springboard for far more Platonic than Stoic digressions and elaborations. While some scholars complain of its lengthiness and tediousness, I find it a fascinating read with plenty of thoughtful insights.

To give but a taste of Simplicius's focus and style, note that he devotes 13 pages of commentary to the first paragraph of Epictetus's *Handbook*.[9] In commenting on the idea that our choices and beliefs

---

9. Refer to this book's Chapter 5.1, which begins by stating that "Some things are under our control, while other things are not under our control."

are up to us and cannot be forced on us from outside, even if sparked or influence by something or someone outside of us, he provides a humorous look at both the pets and the drinking habits of his day:

> Even if we form a judgment this way or that way about it after we've heard something else, providing we do form a judgment, rather than speaking like trained birds (which say, "I drink spiced wine," without knowing what they are saying), this opinion or belief is our own movement; it may sometimes be provoked from the outside or elicited by someone teaching us, but it is not implanted by him.[10]

He also employs some nicely worded elaborations of Epictetus's key thoughts, describing desire, for example, as "a stretching of the soul towards the object of desire."[11] For modern readers who are moved by Epictetus's *Handbook* and would desire to study it more deeply, the modern two-volume translation cited in the last footnote is definitely worth reading and digesting.

The Christianization of Epictetus's *Handbook*

More than one Christian writer thought the moral lessons in Epictetus's *Handbook* were of such potential value to monks that they produced altered, "Christianized" versions, three of which are extant.[12]

The first, referred to by scholars as the Nilus Adaptation, was historically attributed to St. Nilus Ancyranus (d. AD 403), a disciple of St. John Chrysostom, though modern scholars dispute his authorship for many reasons, including the fact that its quality is poor compared to the saint's other authentic works. There are many omissions of words or passages, often when they seem contrary or

10. *Simplicius: On Epictetus's* Handbook 1–26, trans. C. Brittain and T. Brennan (New York: Bloomsbury, 2013), 41.
11. Ibid.
12. These versions, along with the *Handbook* itself, are addressed in a remarkably thorough way in over 400 pages in Gerard Boter's *The Enchiridion of Epictetus and Its Three Christian Adaptations* (Boston: Brill, 1999).

irrelevant to contemporary Christian concerns: for example, references to Diogenes and Heraclitus in chapter 15 and to divination or fortune-telling in chapter 33 have been omitted. Perhaps the most interesting differences in this paraphrase include the omission or substitution of the names of Greek philosophers, most remarkably in chapter 51 with the substitution of the name of St. Paul in the place of Socrates! One example of why the book is considered sub-par next to Nilus's other works involves another such substitution: in chapter 46 "the philosophers" is used instead of the name of Socrates, which renders it pretty nonsensical. (Please recheck point 46 in our last chapter and you'll see what I mean.)

The second Christian version of the *Handbook* is called the *Paraphrasis Christiana*. Of unknown authorship, it was first published along with the *Handbook* itself in London in 1659. Boter details many interesting ways in which the "*Par*" (for short) edition meticulously altered the *Handbook* with Christian monks especially in mind. Indeed, in chapter 29, the word for *philosopher* has been changed to the word for *anchorite* (monk)! The names of Greek philosophers are omitted or changed; and in chapter 51, where the original *Handbook* showed Zeus and Fate, the *Par* replaces them with the Savior and Holy Spirit! Other interesting changes include additions: for example, chapter 11, on interpreting losses as things "given back," flows into commentary on Job 1:21[13]; and chapter 12, on remaining tranquil in spite of a slave boy's transgression, gives rise to a meditation on Matthew 7:3.[14]

The third and final Christianized version of the *Handbook* is called the *Vaticanus graecus* 2231 edition, or *Vat*, for short (or even *V* for shorter still.) Scholars believe it was written sometime between 1317 and 1338. Written in one hand, this version contains similar omissions, additions, and alterations. According to Boter, among the only differences "in comparison with *Nil* and *Par*" is "the choice

---

13. "Naked I came from my mother's womb, and naked shall I return; the LORD gave, and the Lord has taken away: blessed be the name of the Lord" (RSV, Catholic Edition).

14. "Why do you see the speck that is in your brother's eye, but do not notice the log that is in your own eye?" (Ibid.)

of the proper names to replace Socrates and others (Antoninus, Euthymius, Gregorius, Basilius, Arsenius, Solomon)....."[15]

The Renaissance of a Lame Old Man

In 1497, Epictetus's *Handbook* was translated from Greek into Latin in Bologna, Italy. The powerful little book was exceptionally well-received and was soon translated into the other languages of Europe. A host of great Western thinkers (and no doubt some Eastern ones too)[16] since that time have been influenced to some extent by the writings of Epictetus.

Justus Lipsius (1547–1606) of the Netherlands was trained at a Jesuit college and desired to become a novice, but his father did not permit it. He became a professional philologist at the University of Louvain. As for his faith, he became for a time a Lutheran but later returned to Catholicism. His enduring professional interest was in early Roman history and early Roman Stoicism. As for his opinion of "the divine Epictetus," I refer you back to the quotation that was used to begin our chapter 4.

Catholic mathematician and philosopher Blaise Pascal (1623–1662) would praise Epictetus for his commendation of duty and of the primacy of following God, but believed that Epictetus displayed a great arrogance in assuming that man could become virtuous and free of all vice through his own free will and obtain his own happiness without the grace of God.

Catholic mathematician and philosopher Rene Descartes (1596–1650) seemed to deeply appreciate the prolonged and intensive training Epictetus had in mind for any who would even approach virtue and tranquility and freedom from vice and disturbance. In

15. Boter, 260.

16. Jesuit Fr. Matteo Ricci (1552–1610) saw the *Handbook's* affinities with some aspects of Confucianism and had it partially translated into Chinese as an aid in his missionary work. (This is the same man who likewise brought to China the ancient system of memory improvement known as the method of loci [*loci* being Latin for places or locations] invented by Simonides, passed to the West by Cicero and into the realm of Catholic theology through the writings of Saints Albert the Great and Thomas Aquinas.)

his *Discourse on Method,* he laid out maxims by which he would govern his life; his third maxim

> was to try to always conquer my desires rather than change the order of the world, and generally to accustom myself to believe that there is nothing entirely within our control but our own thoughts. . . . I allow, however, that to accustom oneself to regard all things from this point of view requires long exercise and meditation often repeated; and I believe that it is principally in this that is to be found the secret of those philosophers who, in ancient times, were able to free themselves from the empire of fortune, or, despite suffering or poverty, to rival the gods in their happiness.[17]

Epictetus Lands in America
(and Crashes in North Vietnam)

It took the lame old man of Phrygia, Rome, and Nicopolis almost a good millennium and a half to hobble across the Atlantic to the shores of America, but when his ideas arrived they took off running to the very highest of places in academics, literature, and politics. In the will of John Harvard, drawn up in 1638, he bequeathed a copy of Epictetus (presumably the *Handbook*) to the college that bore his name.[18]

A century later, in 1762, an even more famous man, a graduate of William and Mary College, included Epictetus among his recommended reading and ordered a complete Greek text of the entire corpus of Epictetus for the school that he founded, the University of Virginia. He wrote in a letter in 1819, six years before his death: "Epictetus has given us what was good of the Stoics; all beyond, of their dogmas, being hypocrisy and grimace. . . . I have sometimes thought of translating Epictetus (for he has never been tolerably translated into English)."[19] He also wrote that he considered Epicte-

17. As cited in Long, 265.
18. Harvard's university (quite fittingly, Harvard University) would later publish all the extant works of Epictetus and hundreds of other ancient Greek and Latin authors in its extensive Loeb Classical Library, books that are cited many times within these pages.
19. Long, 269.

tus, along with Epicurus, masters in dealing with the self as Jesus is in the duties and the charitable actions that we owe to others. The man's own most famous written work includes early on this rather Epictetan note: "that all men are created equal, that they are endowed by their Creator with certain unalienable Rights, that among these are Life, Liberty, and the pursuit of Happiness." The work is, of course, the Declaration of Independence, and the Epictetus admirer who wrote it was of course, Thomas Jefferson, who would become the third U.S. President.

Famous 19th-century American literary figures who were influenced by Epictetus, or who openly sang his praises for the way that he championed personal liberty, included Ralph Waldo Emerson and Henry David Thoreau. The poet Walt Whitman even told a friend that Epictetus was "one of his own cronies who lasted to this day" and "a universe in himself," and that the day Whitman first read Epictetus "was like being born again."[20]

Epictetus has captured the imagination even of bestselling literary figures of our own time. Tom Wolfe is the author of the multi-million selling novel *Bonfire of the Vanities* (1987). Strange as it may seem, the modern-day impact of the writings of Epictetus forms the core theme of Tom Wolfe's later novel *A Man in Full* (1998). It's a fascinating tale set in southern California and Atlanta, Georgia, in which a young man unjustly imprisoned orders a thriller entitled *The Stoic's Game,* only to be mailed, by mistake, a copy of the works of a real Stoic—Epictetus, that is. He trains himself daily in the wisdom of Epictetus, which gives him internal strength and freedom even while imprisoned; and when his path crosses that of an aging and ailing real-estate tycoon near the end of a life focused only on the externals of money, pleasure, status, and possessions, the tycoon's conversion through Epictetus is so complete that he gives up his wealth and becomes a Stoic televangelist!

Wolfe's work of fiction has been said to have been inspired by a *true* American story with some significant similarities. On September 9, 1965, a U. S. fighter pilot was shot down over a small village in

20. Ibid.

North Vietnam. Three years before, he had been introduced to the writings of Epictetus by a Stanford philosophy professor he happened to meet. The professor told the 38-year-old pilot that as a military man he might find Epictetus of interest, since Fredrick the Great (Fredrick II of Prussia, 1712–1786) never went on a war campaign without it! The pilot was so profoundly moved and changed by Epictetus that, in his own words, as he parachuted out of his disabled airplane he whispered to himself: "Five years down there, at least. I'm leaving the world of technology and entering the world of Epictetus."[21]

The downed pilot underestimated by a bit: he would stay down there, facing torture and unrelenting interrogations as the highest-ranking U.S. officer among many other U.S. prisoners, for more than *seven* years. He would claim that he started out by making "separate files," for what is up to us and what isn't, or for what is under our control and what isn't, as Epictetus's first lesson in the *Handbook* bids us do. He attributed his ability to survive and to encourage his men with this lesson and many others that he learned from Epictetus. He never once even spoke Epictetus's name, but lived and endured each day according to his lessons. Because of the mob-beating he took when he first landed, and the primitive surgery that followed it, his leg was severely broken, and he died in 2005 as what we could call, like his namesake, "a lame old man." Epictetus's doctrines did pass his test, indeed, in his words, "with flying colors."[22] After his release he would become a vice-admiral of the Navy, one of the most decorated war heroes in American history, and almost a Vice-President of the United States of America when he ran as Ross Perot's running mate in 1992. This true American and epic Epictetan hero was a man named James Bond Stockdale.

21. J.B. Stockdale, *Courage Under Fire: Testing Epictetus' Doctrines in a Laboratory of Human Behavior* (Stanford: Hoover Institution, 1993), 7.

22. Ibid., 18.

From the Porch to the Couch:
Epictetus in Modern Cognitive Psychotherapy

Since the early 1960s there has been another very common way in which Americans and Europeans may stumble across Epictetus. Indeed, it happened to me during my undergraduate studies as a psychology major. To make a long story very short, I came to find that in the late 1950s psychotherapist Albert Ellis (1913–2007) became dissatisfied with the benefit to his patients from Freudian psychotherapy in which he sat behind them on a couch, scribbling notes while they recalled their childhoods and expounded upon all their problems. He felt the desire to get them off the couch, to sit with them eye to eye, to rationally converse with his patients and to give them sound advice. He had come to believe that *what was causing their emotional distress was not nearly so much some trauma from childhood as what they kept retelling themselves about their traumas as adults.* He recalled that in his personal life, as a young man he had overcome an intense fear of his own (the fear of speaking to girls, of all things) by what he had learned from the writings of Epictetus!

Now, speaking of fear and of speaking, many who have written about Epictetus attest to the help of his wisdom in their own lives, so I'll ask your forbearance as I join their number. In the *Discourses* Epictetus specifically addresses the greatest fear of my own youth, a fear some say is the most widespread of them all—the fear of public speaking! Indeed, even into my college years I would sit in fear and trembling when a professor announced that we would be required to give a speech, calculating the odds that he or she might get ill and the speech requirement would go by the wayside. When I spoke before an audience my face would flush, my voice would falter, and my heart would race inside my chest. Epictetus said the speaker becomes anxious when he focuses not on the matter of his speech (which is under his control) but the possible reactions of his audience (which is not). So, once as a college senior, when my psychology professor remained in good health all term, I had no choice but to give a talk. I started by asking my classmates' pardon if they could see my heart pounding within my chest, and then I just got on with it. Now, thanks to Ellis and Epictetus, I give talks to all sorts of audiences with scarcely a flutter, by focusing only on what's under my control, like doing my homework before giving the talk![23]

So, what was the fundamental Epictetan insight that would become the foundation of what Ellis would call Rational-Emotive Therapy, and later Rational-Emotive-Behavior Therapy? It comes from the *Handbook*'s chapter 5:*"People are disturbed not by things, but by the view they take of things."* Taking this concept and running with it, Ellis elaborated a complete and effective system of psychotherapy that retrains patients to examine their judgments and to challenge and change the disturbing ways they talk to themselves, attributing their emotions to external causes. Perhaps the most fundamental kernel of Ellis's adaptation of Epictetus's insight is his "ABC theory of emotions." It really is as easy as ABC (well, and also D and E). Allow me, then, to paraphrase one of Ellis's own examples, this one about the control not of fear but of anger.

Let's say a huge man steps on your foot as he passes by you in a crowded bus, and without a word of apology. Might you be angry? It seems like a clear-cut case of the old stimulus-response (S-R) psychology. The stimulus (S) of the huge man's step upon your foot has immediately produced the response (R) of your pain and anger. After all, haven't you frequently told people, *"You* made me angry!"? However, modern cognitive psychologists have pointed out that something actually does go on between the "S" and the "R." They label this the "O," standing for organism. Our minds are not empty, black boxes. Something goes on inside us between the big guy's heel, our painful foot, and our angry reaction; between someone's hurtful action and our own angry response.

Ellis built upon the ideas of Stoics, primarily Epictetus, and rear-

23. Once, around the year 2000, I was blessed with the opportunity to sit "at the feet of the master," when Ellis himself gave a talk at Bradley University in Peoria, Illinois. A friend found out about the talk at the last minute, and after more than an hour's drive we were disappointed when we were told no seats were left when we arrived—until they told us that Ellis didn't mind if we sat at his feet at the edge of the stage. We didn't mind either. (In fact, my wife would later jokingly ask if we'd kissed them!)

ranged the alphabet in a very simple way to explain our emotional reactions to outside events. So then, to make it as easy as ABC, the stimulus (S) becomes the "activating event" (A); the response (R) becomes the emotional or behavioral "consequence" (C); and the organism (O) is refined and renamed "belief" (B), because that is the main thing that goes on in our minds between the external event and our own reactions. Abstract enough? Then let's make it as simple as ABC by reframing our little scenario a bit.

Let's say that a huge man steps on your foot as he passes you in a crowded bus without a word of apology (A). Might you be angry (C)? It is time to call in the (B), for it is *beliefs* that can serve to conquer our own excessive anger. What if you then noticed the man's dark glasses and white cane? Your foot might still hurt like the dickens, but would you still be *angry* with him? Chances are you would not, because your belief about him would change. You would no longer tell yourself what a knave he is, but might tell yourself how noble he is to get out and travel alone despite his blindness, praying that God might give you such grace should you be in the same position.

However, modern systems of psychotherapy and ancient Stoic philosophical techniques go much deeper than this in their remedies against anger. What if that big dude was not blind and actually enjoys crunching people's toes? Must we still feel angry at him and upset ourselves about his action? More accurately stated, must we *make ourselves* angry and upset? Ellis and Epictetus emphatically answer "No!" When we get angry, we tend to rile ourselves up further in our self-talk, ruminating on our pain and on the injustice of whatever kind of insult we believed we have suffered.

The use of our faculty of reason to rein in emotions like anger adds another letter to our alphabetic arsenal, namely "D," for disputation of beliefs. When we dispute automatic beliefs that produce anger in our souls, we may then go on to exchange a sinful "C" for a virtuous new "E" (emotional consequence.) Let's lay it out nice and simple, for our little example:

The ABCs of Emotional Disturbance (And Healing)

A	B	C	D	E
Activating Event	Beliefs (Irrational)	Emotional Consequence	Disputation of Beliefs (leading to new, rational beliefs	New Emotional Consequence
Big guy steps on foot. (He is blind.)	"The careless oaf should watch his step! I'd like to get even with him somehow."	Anger	"He's blind. It was an accident. How courageous for him to travel alone."	Forgiveness and adoration
Big guy steps on foot. (Not blind. Done on purpose.)	"The careless oaf should watch his step! I'd like to get even with him somehow."	Anger	"What a sorry thing for a grown man to think that is appropriate. I'll pray for him."	Forgiveness and compassion, along with reasonable annoyance

So here we see in practice, more than 18 centuries after Epictetus, a modern revival and extension of some of his fundamental thoughts on maintaining mental health.[24] Not long after Ellis's early publications on Rational-Emotive Therapy, an American psychiatrist, Aaron Beck (b. 1921), developed the system of Cognitive Therapy with the same fundamental Epictetan principles, though his early prominence came from his book on the treatment of depression, and he and his followers developed some unique additional methods of therapy that have often proven quite successful.[25] Modern systems of psychotherapy building on Ellis and Beck's ideas are

24. Some moderns note that while the modern cognitive therapies are perfectly consistent with the Stoic principles for the removal of disturbance, they do not inculcate the positive goal of a life of virtue. Further, while we have seen Epictetus's devout piety, Ellis was a vocal atheist.

25. After all, Epictetus did say the philosopher's school is a hospital! Ellis's seminal work was *Reason and Emotion in Psychotherapy: A New and Comprehensive Method of Treating Human Disturbances* (New York: Citadel Press, 1962); and Beck's was *Cognitive Therapy of Depression* (New York: Guilford Press, 1967).

generically called "cognitive behavior therapies," and many modern theoreticians and practitioners have penned books that pay due homage to the lame old man on the porch.[26]

Start or Renew Your Own Epictetan Legacy

Whitman said that reading Epictetus, "a universe in himself," was like being born again. Lipsius said the brilliant Epictetus stirred his soul and seemed ever new, no matter how often he returned to him. If you have not yet read Epictetus and entered into his brilliant universe, I envy you the rejuvenating trip. If you have, then find time to go back and sit upon Epictetus's "porch," reopen Arrian's pages, and let God's lame messenger stir your soul once more.

26. Excellent examples include Donald Robertson's *The Philosophy of Cognitive-Behavioral Therapy (CBT): Stoic Philosophy as Rational and Cognitive Psychotherapy* (London: Karnac Books, 2010) and Arthur Still and Windy Dryden's *The Historical and Philosophical Context of Rational Psychotherapy: The Legacy of Epictetus* (London, Karnac Books, 2012).

PART III

Seneca:
Silver-Tongued Stoic Stylist

✠

Philosophy has the single task of discovering the truth about the divine and human worlds. The religious conscience, the sense of duty, justice and all the rest of the close-knit, interdependent "company of virtues," never leave her side. Philosophy has taught men to worship what is divine, to love what is human, telling us that with the gods belong authority, and among human beings fellowship.

∽Seneca, *Letter* 90[1]

1. Seneca, *Letters from a Stoic* (New York: Penguin Books, 1969) 162.

7
The Life of the Rich Man Who Sought Higher Treasures

Someone has made a joke about the baldness of my head, the weakness of my eyes, the thinness of my legs, the shortness of my stature; what insult is there in telling me what everybody sees?

⁓Lucius Annaeus Seneca[1]

I am not a wise man, nor—to feed your malevolence!—shall I ever be. And so require not from me that I should be equal to the best, but that I should be better than the wicked. It is enough for me if every day I reduce the number of my vices, and blame my mistakes.... What I say is not spoken on my own behalf—for I am sunk in deep vice of every kind—but on behalf of the man who has actually achieved something.

⁓Lucius Annaeus Seneca[2]

Seneca, the great Roman Stoic whose lifespan intersected those of both Musonius Rufus and Epictetus, differed from those philosophers in so many drastic ways. While they spoke Greek and their philosophical legacy comes down to us in Greek, Seneca spoke and wrote in Latin. While we have but small samples of their wisdom, passed down second-hand through the writings of others, Seneca was a most prolific writer with a good number of volumes extant in our day. While we cannot quote Musonius Rufus and Epictetus

---

1. Cited in Richard Mott Gummere, *Seneca the Philosopher and His Modern Message* (Bibliobazaar, 2008), 54. (Originally published in 1922.)
2. "On the Happy Life" in *Seneca's Moral Essays, Volume II*, trans. John W. Basore (Cambridge, MA: Harvard University Press), 143–45.

directly in any autobiographical comments, we can in the case of Seneca. While the former two were professional teachers of philosophy, the latter was primarily a very successful politician and courtier. Philosophy was never his vocation, but a lifelong avocation. While Epictetus refers to Musonius several times in his writing, no references to Seneca survive in either man's work; and neither does Seneca reference either of them.

This is intriguing, especially since Rufus and Seneca were both of the equestrian order in Rome, and since Epaphroditus, Epictetus's one-time owner, was a secretary to Nero—indeed, as we saw, the man who eventually killed him at his own request to avoid the blows of the soldiers who had been ordered to beat the tyrant to death with clubs. Seneca, as we will see, was for years Nero's tutor and senior adviser. Perhaps there are political reasons, since Rufus was more aligned with the senators who held to the old Roman republican tradition, while Seneca was so closely aligned to the rule of the emperors. Perhaps they walked in different political worlds, as different as the different linguistic worlds of Greek and Latin in which they chose to practice philosophy. Perhaps there are other reasons, and maybe they even did reference each other in works that no longer exist, or in lost works which may one day be found.

In any event, there is even a far greater difference. Both Musonius and Epictetus were considered by all who knew them to be men of the greatest integrity. Seneca, on the contrary, was considered by some a great hypocrite, indeed, the prime example of a man who did *not* practice what he preached to others: the rich man who praised poverty, the lustful man who counseled self-control, the proud man who feigned humility. As we will see in the sections that follow, it is almost as if there were two Senecas, the rich, powerful, and conniving politician, and the humble, noble man of letters and of high-minded moral philosophy. Indeed, various contemporaries and historians, and centuries of later thinkers, have argued on both sides that the one or the other represents the real Seneca.

Nonetheless, how fascinating it is that despite the vast universe of differences in the lives of this Roman Stoic and the two sages we have met thus far, the messages they preached were extremely consistent, as if they came from the same Sender. All sang the praises of a life guided by philosophy, in pursuit of virtue and the highest of goods, by following God, focusing only on things within our control, and honoring all men and women as brothers and sisters. It will be up to the reader to form his or her own opinion as to what extent Seneca was a most artful hypocrite, or perhaps an honest and genuine man who truly sought to practice what he preached about a life devoted to philosophy and virtue, but who was hemmed in, overwhelmed, and eventually extinguished by the noxious, notorious, and nearly inescapable environment he placed himself in through his youthful passion for worldly success.

A Life of Intrigue and Luxury

Lucius Annaeus Seneca was born in 4 BC in *Corduba* (Cordoba or Cordova), in the south of the long-held Roman Province of *Hispania* (Spain). His father, often referred to as "Seneca the Elder," was a respected rhetorician and a *procurator* who managed the finances of the province for Rome. His mother was named Helvia. Like Musonius Rufus, Seneca was born into the equestrian or knightly order, one tier below that of the senatorial class. Our Seneca was the second of three sons. The eldest was Lucius Anneas Novatus, later known as L. Junios Gallio Anneanas, who attained lasting fame for his mention in the New Testament.[3] The youngest was Marcus Annaeus Mela, who shunned the political life, was once declared by their father to be the smartest of the three,[4] and was himself the father of the famous Roman poet Lucan (Marcus Annaeus Lucanus, to be precise).

The family moved to Rome when our Seneca was young and he grew up immersed in the culture, politics, and philosophy at Rome, though he did not confine himself to that city. His uncle was the governor of Egypt and he visited there often, studying its geogra-

---

3. In Acts 18:12–17 we read how Gallio, the Roman proconsul of Achaia, refused to stand in judgment of St. Paul when a group of Jews brought Paul before him on charges of unlawful worship of God.

4. Seneca the Elder was a staunch conservative of the old Roman school, disdainful of foreign influences, including Greek philosophy.

phy, its customs, and its religion, and writing a book about it. He long retained an interest in natural history and geography, indicating a broader range of interests than our other Roman Stoic moralists.

Seneca's youth was also marked by bouts of pour health, especially from asthma, it seems. He experienced such severe attacks of loss of breath that he described them as "preparations for death." He even admitted to thoughts of suicide at times, which he would not pursue out of concern for his father. Alexandria, Egypt was at the crossroads of the East and the West, and Seneca came in contact with the most influential Eastern ideas of his day. He dabbled for a time in Pythagorean mystical philosophy.

By the time he attained young adulthood, Seneca's family's connections and his own obvious talents as a thinker and speaker brought him a series of increasingly important public offices, with the wealth to go along with them. His first big position was the *quaestorship*, a job in charge of financial affairs which he attained while in his thirties, around the year AD 33. Seneca and his family were apparently in the good graces of the Emperor Augustus and his successor Tiberius. Seneca entered the senatorial ranks and became known for his unique style and power as an orator, and this may be why the cruel and unstable Caligula railed at Seneca virtually as soon as he became Emperor in the year 37. Historians have reported that Caligula spared Seneca the death penalty only when told that Seneca's health was so poor that he'd probably die soon of natural causes anyway.

After Caligula was murdered in 41 and his uncle Claudius was named emperor, Seneca drew the ire of Claudius's beautiful and spiteful wife Messalina, perhaps because of his brilliance, and certainly because of his sympathy for Caligula's sisters, whom she considered threats. Messalina persuaded Claudius to banish Seneca to the island of Corsica on the vague and questionable charge of adultery with Julia Livia, one of Caligula's sisters. Corsica is a rather large island, over 100 miles long and 50 miles wide, to the west of Italy and southeast of France. Seneca's banishment lasted 8 years, from the age of 45 to 53. He spent much of this time writing tragedies, nine of which we still possess today.

In the year 49, political winds had changed, and another sister of Caligula, the beautiful and calculating Agrippina, recalled Seneca to Rome to tutor her young son, one Lucius Domitius Ahenobarbus, far better known later on as the bloodthirsty Emperor Nero Caesar. Agrippina had displaced the now dead Messalina as Claudius's bride and arranged for herself the lofty title of *Augusta*.[5] After Claudius's death, and the untimely and unnatural demise of Claudius and Messalina's natural son Britannicus, Agrippina had arranged for the ascension of Nero, her son from a previous marriage. For more than a decade the elegant and prudent Seneca, along with the stern and plainspoken military leader Burrus, kept young Nero pretty much in line and maintained harmony within the empire. A later Emperor, Trajan, would call the first five years of Nero's reign under Seneca's guidance "golden years" in the history of Rome; but as Nero matured, he gradually shook off the restraints of his mentors, let his passions run wild, and heaped evil upon evil. One of the earliest and grossest of young Nero's evil deeds was to secretly order the death of his own mother Agrippina, aged 43, in the year 59. His first attempt failed when she swam free of a ship he'd ordered to be rigged to sink, so he ordered his sailors to do it by the sword, disclaiming any personal responsibility. Historians debate to what extent Seneca may have been aware of and looked away from his young protégé's act of matricide.

When Burrus died in 62, the balance of power had shifted, as new, far less scrupulous advisers entered the scene; and Seneca sought to be free from the court life in Rome. He traveled around Italy to his many rich and sumptuous villas, composing books of natural history and writing the famous letters to his friend Lucilius that we'll highlight in our next chapter. By the year 65, many in Rome had had all they could take of Nero's antics: the murders of any he suspected of seeking his demise; and his gallivanting about the Mediterranean entering musical competitions in which he played his lyre and recited his own poetry, sometimes for hours on

---

5. The female equivalent of the Emperor's esteemed title of *Augustus,* a title even higher than that of *Caesar.*

end, despite Seneca's urgings not to do so, and complete with a large corps of a traveling audience, trained to clap in choreographed rhythms for the effete musician who ruled the civilized world. (Somehow, he never failed to win first prize.) There was also the matter of the burning of Rome in the year 64. Some claimed that Nero had started it and that he plucked on the strings of his lyre, singing a song of the burning of Troy while watching Rome burn.

In the year 65, not long before his own inglorious death, Nero charged that Seneca was complicit in a conspiracy that sought to assassinate Nero and make emperor a senator named Gaius Calpurnius Piso. Some, including perhaps Seneca himself, believed that when Piso's role was discovered, Seneca himself might become the new Emperor, like Plato's philosopher-king, should Nero still be assassinated. Seneca, however, was ordered by Nero to take his own life. Seneca had often written about the life and the death of Socrates, the man esteemed as a sage by our Roman Stoics. Socrates did not fear death, and willingly drank his drought of hemlock. Seneca had anticipated this order and had poison prepared for his use. He chose, however, to open the veins in his arm with a knife to let his life force slowly ebb away. His wife Paulina chose to share this same fate with him. He bled slowly, however, and proceeded to slice open veins behind his knees as well. Suffering in pain, and yet failing to lose consciousness, Seneca then drank the poison, but due to the loss of blood and slow circulation, it did not take effect. He retired to a separate room, so he and his wife would not witness each other's dying agonies. He placed himself in a hot, steamy bath, slowly bleeding and suffocating until his spirit left his body.

A Life in Pursuit of Wisdom

Seneca certainly knew vast wealth and power, and every kind of luxury. Some throughout the ages, fueled in part by the writings of the third century historian Dio Cassius, have called him the ultimate hypocrite. They note as well the self-serving qualities apparent even in some of his own moral writings: inserting phrases, for example, to flatter the current emperor to his own advantage. A fascinating recent study[6] highlights the two very different views of Seneca as hypocrite or enlightened sage (the latter more consistent with his portrayal in the writings of the first-century historian Tacitus) by the two most famous statues that represent him. There is an old Roman bust of a rugged, somewhat haggard, bearded man, unearthed in Herculaneum, Italy[7] that was long thought to portray Seneca. It inspired paintings by the likes of Rubens and David, and it can be seen on the covers of some modern books about Seneca. It is now known, however, as the false or "Pseudo-Seneca," since an actual portrait bust of Seneca was unearthed in Rome in the year 1813. This third-century bust is two-sided, depicting Seneca facing in one direction and Socrates behind him facing the opposite direction. The fact that Seneca is depicted as the twin of Socrates should say something of the esteem in which he was held. This Seneca, however, is neither bearded nor haggard, but is bald and clean-shaven, with heavy jowls, looking more like a seeker of softness and luxury than an ascetic seeker of wisdom.

We should recall, nonetheless, how Seneca describes himself in the quotation at the head of this chapter. What insult was there if a sculptor sculpted that which everyone sees? After all, not all philosophers need look alike. St. Thomas Aquinas too was neither slim nor bearded. To immerse oneself in the study of the *Letters* and *Moral Essays* of Seneca is to immerse oneself in a lofty, refined, and caring spirit, the equal of Musonius and Epictetus in its call to virtue and goodness and its love for the pursuit of wisdom. Seneca, by his own admission, was no philosophical sage, but only a man who sincerely sought wisdom. I find it hard to believe that he was not sincere. Yes, he was a rich man who praised poverty; but in order to be free of Nero's court, he was ready to give all that he possessed to the Emperor himself. Surely tempted by the wealth, Nero probably realized how mean and greedy he would appear to the world if he took the old Stoic up on his offer.

6. James Romm, *Dying Every Day: Seneca at the Court of Nero* (New York: Alfred A. Knopf, 2014).

7. A town, like Pompeii, devastated by the eruption of Mt. Vesuvius in AD 79.

The Porch and the Cross

Seneca choose to try to combine the life of a powerful politician with that of a philosopher, and it appears that when he crossed not the Rubicon but the Tiber, he found himself forever unable to retreat. I invite readers to form their own opinions of the man who was Seneca by absorbing his own writings, particular the *Letters* he wrote in the last few years of his life. He praises retirement, discourages seeking office and power, sings the praises of the life philosophic, and displays again and again true humility and humor.

Writing in his 60s, he considered himself to have attained old age (and he would never live to see 70). In *Letter* 64, he tells his friend Lucilius the signs that he sees of his advancing age. He visits his old country estate and finds the old house in a state of dilapidation. This is the house that grew under his own hands, and yet stones of his age are crumbling to pieces! He scolds the caretaker for the state of a row of trees that are gnarled and shriveled and bear no leaves. He tells them they need to have the ground under them loosened and they must be watered. The caretaker tells him he has done all that, but to not avail, because the trees are simply old. (Seneca lets us in on his secret that he himself had planted those trees!) He then asks the caretaker about the identity of a rickety old slave who comes into view, a man who looks like he's knocking at death's door. The old man himself replies to Seneca: "Don't you know me, sir? I am Felicio; you used to bring me little images. My father was Philositus the steward, and I am your pet slave."[8] Seneca says the man is crazy, or has become a boy again, since his teeth are falling out (but he knows that the slave tells the truth)!

Seneca muses that the old country homestead of his youth revealed to him his age wherever he turned—but he is not despondent. Rather, he urges us to love and to cherish our old age:

> Fruits are most welcome when almost over; youth is most charming at its close; the last drink delights the toper,—the glass which souses him and puts the finishing touch on his drunkenness. Each pleasure reserves to the end the greatest delights which it contains.

8. Seneca, *Epistles* 1-65, trans. R. Gummere (Cambridge, MA: Harvard University Press), 67.

Life is most delightful when it is on the downward slope, but has not yet reached the decline. . . . How comforting it is to have tired out one's appetites, and to have done with them![9]

Let's move on now to see what lessons this second "lame old man" can give us to make the most of our own years, whether we are still on the upward slope or have started down the other side!

9. Ibid., 69.

8

Lessons Eloquent, Elegant, and Worldly-Wise

Philosophy's power to blunt all the blows of circumstances is beyond belief. Never a single missile lodges in her; she has strong, impenetrable defenses; some blows she breaks the force of, parrying them with the slack of her gown as if they were trivial, others she flings off and hurls back at the sender.

~Seneca, *Letter* 53[1]

Considered en masse, the letters form a fruitful and helpful handbook, of the very widest scope and interest.
~Richard M. Gummere on Seneca's *Letters to Lucilius*[2]

SENECA IS AS WORLDLY, studied, and polished as Epictetus is earthy, blunt, and unadorned; yet both the imperious imperial adviser and the humble son of a slave, in their different voices, sing very similar songs in praise of the beauty and the power of philosophy. In this chapter we will see Stoicism through the eyes not of a professional teacher like Musonius Rufus or Epictetus, but of a man completely embroiled in the nitty-gritty politics and conflicts of life at the highest of levels of worldly power and influence. We will focus on lessons Seneca provided in his *Letters* or *Epistles* addressed to his somewhat younger friend Lucilius, but clearly intended for posterity for ages to come, including you and me.

---

1. *Letters from a Stoic*, 103.
2. Seneca, *Epistles* 1–65, xiii.

With the few surviving second-hand lectures of Rufus, we were able to summarize all twenty-one of them in our chapter 2. Thanks to Arrian's rendering of Epictetus's condensed *Handbook*, we were able to quickly take in all of its fifty-three lessons. Seneca's surviving works are far more vast, containing many times more words than our previous two Stoics put together (along with the works of Marcus Aurelius as well). In this chapter we will survey but a dozen samples of the 124 letters, some quite lengthy,[3] penned by Seneca himself during the last three years of his life. At times I will point them out, but I ask readers to remain attentive to some common Stoic themes in discussing which Seneca parallels his peer Musonius Rufus and presages Epictetus, who would begin to teach not too many years after Seneca's death. I advise you as well to be on the lookout for lessons that *you* might find helpful today—literally, today; for Seneca advises Lucilius to "hold every hour in your grasp. Lay hold of to-day's task, and you will not need to depend so much upon to-morrow's."[4]

Letter 2:
How to Read Books Wisely

Seneca's very first letter to Lucilius was an admonition to value his time and use it wisely. The second letter makes clear that Lucilius's time will be spent wisely in reading good books, but only if he reads selectively. Seneca praises his friend for not distracting himself by moving unnecessarily from place to place, because such restlessness reveals a disordered mind. A well-ordered mind can rest in one place, and a well-ordered man can "linger in his own company."[5] Such a calm, well-ordered man will be wise also to linger in the company of a limited number of masterful authors, rather than to collect and half-read too many books of all sorts. As a person who travels all the time meets many people but establishes few lasting friendships, so too the man who reads too many different books

---

3. The Harvard University Press Loeb Classical Library edition with Latin text and English translations requires three separate volumes totaling over 1,400 pages, including scholarly apparatus.

4. Seneca, *Epistles* 1–65, 3.

5. Seneca, *Epistles* 1–65, 7.

will digest and make his own very little lasting wisdom. To desire to dip into too many books at once is to be like the finicky eater who nibbles a bit of this and then a bit of that without taking in substantial nourishment.

Seneca advises Lucilius to read frequently from a limited cadre of established master authors who can provide real food for the spirit. If he desires a change of pace, he should go back and reread from the wisest he has read before. He should strive too, each day, to draw out some lesson that will fortify him against poverty, death, and all kinds of misfortunes, and then to chew on that nugget of wisdom throughout the day. Seneca then offers such a nugget of wisdom, not from a Stoic philosopher, but from Epicurus, the philosopher known best for championing pleasure: "Contented poverty is an honourable estate."[6] Seneca elaborates that there is no poverty where one feels contentment, and he offers his own bon mot: "It is not the man who has little who is poor, but the one who hankers after more."[7]

Letter 5:
How the Philosopher Deals with Popular Culture

Seneca congratulates Lucilius on making the sacrifices necessary to pursue the study of philosophy and to strive every day to become a better person. Indeed, he does not merely encourage him to continue, but begs and implores him to do so. He advises him, though, to be sure to avoid attention-seeking behaviors as he strives for self-betterment. He urges him not to do things like grow his hair exceedingly long, make a show of wearing shabby clothing, or openly proclaim his disdain of riches. The lives of philosophers should not be *opposed* to the lives of the masses, but marked by the pursuit of *higher* goods. The student of philosophy should be in outward appearance like his fellow man, but inwardly different

6. Ibid., 9. (Seneca will make clear in several later letters that Epicurus, though not of their school, is one of the masters of philosophy whose books he returns to time and again.)

7. *Letters from a Stoic*, 34.

because of the true goods he seeks. Seneca urges moderation in matters of outward appearance: for example, dressing neither gaudily nor shabbily but in conformance with the norms of one's circles. The first thing philosophy should bring us is a feeling of benevolent fellowship and community with all of mankind, so the philosopher should not hold in disdain or alienate those whom he would seek to help. If the life of the philosopher is shown to be too strange or too harsh, the public will have no interest in sharing it. To live in accordance with nature is to live simply, and in a way that others can understand and hopefully seek to emulate.

Does this mean that we should live no differently than the masses? Not at all. Anyone entering our homes should be aware that we are different. They should admire us rather than our furnishings and possessions. A great man treats simple earthenware as if it were silver. A man who owns silver and treats it as earthenware is no less great. "It is the sign of an unstable mind not to be able to endure riches."[8]

Seneca closes this letter, as he does most of them, with a simple lesson he has acquired through his daily readings, this time from the Stoic Hecato of Rhodes (first/second centuries BC), who wrote, "Cease to hope and you will cease to fear." He explains that these two seemingly different emotions both produce anxiety by stretching our minds toward the future, rather than teaching us to adapt ourselves to the present. This changes the great human blessing of the power of foresight into a self-imposed curse. Animals flee from dangers they actually see, but stop worrying once they escape. We, however, needlessly torment ourselves with dread of what has already passed and with fear of what is yet to come. Live in the present and you will not be disturbed or unhappy.

Letter 7:
How the Philosopher Faces Spectacles and Crowds

Lucilius asked Seneca what he should be careful to avoid, and Seneca answers, "crowds." We are easily influenced by others, and massive crowds encourage vices either directly or subtly and uncon-

8. Seneca, *Epistles* 1–65, 23.

sciously.[9] The worst kind of crowd in the first century of the Roman Empire was the crowd at the gladiatorial games. One would come home from such spectacles more selfish, cruel, and inhuman. Seneca talks about stopping in during the lunch hour, hoping to find some relaxing, light-hearted entertainment to provide relief from the morning's bloodshed and gore, but finds it is even more cruel and sadistic. Here he sees not trained and armored gladiators but criminals pitted against one another without a bit of armor to protect them from excruciating blows and stabs. In the morning men are thrown to lions and bears; but at noon they are thrown to the spectators, many of whom prefer such butchery. Spectators expect every last criminal to die at each other's hands, save for the lone survivor who will still face some other form of savage execution. "Kill him! Beat him! Burn him!" they cheer, as they ask among themselves why some man seems so cowardly or unwilling to murder his foe. Some will defend their actions, saying that these men are murderers. Seneca retorts rhetorically to a spectator: "Granted that as a murderer he deserved this punishment, what have you done, you wretched fellow, to deserve to watch it?"[10]

We are influenced by the company we keep. Even men like Socrates or Cato might have been shaken had they spent their time among the unthinking multitude. A single example of vice can harm us. One friend with luxurious habits can lead us to grow soft and flabby. Never underestimate, then, the powerful influence of a mob. The student of philosophy should learn to be content retiring within himself and seeking out the company both of those who can lift him up and improve him and of those whom he might be capable of improving. After all, people learn as they teach.

Seneca ends this letter with three pearls of wisdom to encourage Lucilius (and us) to abandon the need for approval from the majority, and I'll provide but the second one here. An anonymous person, when once asked why he was working so hard crafting some object that only a few would ever see, replied, "A few is enough for me; so is

---

9. As I write (on April 28, 2015), a state of emergency has been declared in Baltimore, Maryland, in response to the danger of the crowd and mob action.

10. *Letters from a Stoic*, 42.

one; and so is none."[11] One's good qualities should face inwards, not outwards.

Letter 13:
On Conquering Needless Fears

Seneca compliments Lucilius on the spirit he has shown in grappling with Fortune, even before he began to equip himself with wholesome philosophical maxims that can be used to overcome obstacles. Facing difficulties is what makes us strong and builds virtue in us:

> No prizefighter can go with high spirits into the strife if he has never been beaten black and blue; the only contestant who can confidently enter the lists is the man who has seen his own blood, who has felt his teeth rattle beneath his opponent's fist, who has been tripped and felt the full force of his adversary's charge, who has been downed in body but not in spirit, one who, as often as he falls, rises again with greater defiance than ever.[12]

Remembering that facing adversity makes us stronger can help us conquer three classes of fears: (1) fears that bother us more than they really ought, (2) fears that bother us before they ought, and (3) fears that should not bother us at all. This can inoculate against those who would try to blunt our happiness by making us focus on bad things that may or may not happen. One should train oneself to examine one's fears, to make sure they are not exaggerated; and to make sure one does not forsake living in the present for fear of what may or may not ever happen. One should not tell oneself that the worst will not happen, but rather say to oneself, "Well, what if it does happen? Let us see who wins! Perhaps it happens for my best interest; it may be that such a death will shed credit upon my life."[13]

Seneca ends the letter with his usual maxim, this yet another from Epicurus, to the effect that the foolish person is always just getting ready to live. He calls to mind men who even in old age are

11. Ibid., 44.
12. *Epistles,* 74–75.
13. Ibid., 83.

constantly seeking new external goals, planning to embark on new endeavors like a run for political office or to start a new business rather than living each and every day in accordance with nature.

Letter 15:
A Sound Mind in a Sound Body

Seneca writes to Lucilius of the old Roman habit of beginning letters with the salutation to the effect that "If you are well, all is well, and I am well," suggesting that perhaps it would be better to start his letters by saying, "If you are studying philosophy, it is well."[14] Seneca counsels that a man should not devote too much time to caring for his body, because regardless of how powerful and muscular a man may become, he'll never be a match for a first-class bull! Further, constant overfeeding dulls the mind; and there is much more to life than eating and sweating!

Seneca was certainly not one to pooh-pooh all exercise, however. He goes on as follows:

> Now there are short and simple exercises which tire the body rapidly, and so save our time; and time is something of which we ought to keep strict account. These exercises are running, brandishing weights, and jumping.... But whatever you do, come back soon from body to mind. The mind must be exercised both day and night.[15]

He tells Lucilius he does not intend for him to live bent over his books and his writing implements, but to intersperse reading and riding with bouts of mild exercise like walking or riding, in addition to the higher-intensity exercises he mentioned above. Seneca then

14. Ibid., 97. (*Si philipharis, bene est,* or, in another translation [*Letters of a Stoic*, 60], "I trust this finds you in pursuit of wisdom.")

15. Ibid., 99. (I couldn't help but include this quotation from Seneca in my own book *Fit for Eternal Life* when I detailed the methods of modern High Intensity Training [HIT], strength training specifically formulated for simple, brief, intense, and infrequent workout that provide maximum growth stimulation with a minimal investment in time!)

moves into a discussion of hopes and desires in a manner not unlike Epictetus:

> Away with fripperies which only serve for show! As to what the future's uncertain lot has in store, why should I demand of Fortune that she give, rather than demand of myself that I should not crave?[16]

Letter 16:
How Philosophy Builds the Soul

Here we find a brief paean to philosophy as a guide to life and happiness. Seneca assures Lucilius that no one can lead a happy life without philosophy, and even those just beginning in the pursuit of wisdom will find that their lives thereby become much more bearable. He advises his friend to continue his daily reflections and reminds him that *keeping* noble resolutions is more important than *making* them.[17] Through daily perseverance, his studies will soon become an entrenched habit.

Philosophy is not something for which one should seek attention or amusement. Philosophy is not matter of words, but of facts. It molds and builds the soul; it orders our life, guides our actions, shows us what we should do and also what we shouldn't. Philosophy sits at the helm and guides our course through life. Some might ask how philosophy is of any use if Fate exists, if God rules the universe, or if all things are a matter of Chance. Seneca answers that philosophy still prevails: "She will encourage us to obey God cheerfully, but Fortune defiantly; she will teach us to follow God and endure Chance."[18] Therefore, Seneca exhorts his friend not to allow his spiritual impulse for wisdom to grow weak or cold, but to establish it solidly so that what is now an impulse will become a firm habit of mind.

16. Ibid., 103.

17. As I write (on January 3, 2015), I recall how I had to circle my gym's parking lot before I could find a space this morning, so full it was of the cars of New Year's "resolutionists." Doubting that most will heed wise Seneca's advice, I feel confident that I will park again in ease within about a month!

18. *Epistles,* 107.

He ends again with an exhortation to drop all desires for external goods and luxuries. Natural desires are limited, but those that spring from false impressions never satisfy and have no limits at all.[19]

Letter 20:
Philosophy Not Spoken, but Lived

Philosophy does not seek to make speeches or entertain crowds with high-sounding word-play; it teaches us how to act, not how to talk about acting. It teaches every man that his deeds must match his words and that his inner life and outer life must always be in harmony. Philosophers, in other words, must walk their talk and practice what they preach. This is no easy task and is achieved only through rigorous self-examination. Observe yourself, says Seneca: Are your manner of clothing and your housing consistent with your philosophy? Are you generous toward yourself and stingy with your family? Do you eat frugal meals, but maintain a massive, ostentatious house? You should regulate yourself by one and the same norm in all your affairs. You should not be like those who control themselves at home but then strut about in public. "What is wisdom? Always desiring the same things, and always refusing the same things."[20] It goes without saying that what you wish should be right, because if it was not right it could not always satisfy.

Seneca also recommends a practical exercise to Lucilius to train him in desiring only what is right and in accordance with nature. He says it is not necessary for the philosopher to renounce all his possessions, but it is a good thing to practice voluntary poverty and simplicity at times for a few days, preparing oneself and rehearsing, as it were, should true poverty befall one. Indeed, he says this can be a pleasant experience that provides a sense of freedom from the care for unneeded things. This can rouse the soul from its sleep and remind it that nature's true needs are very few. Seneca ends with a picturesque and humorous description of the way that we all get

---

19. Cf. chapter 39 of Epictetus's *Handbook* on the true measure of shoes!

20. *Epistles,* 135. (Recall Epictetus's philosophical training in desires and aversions.)

our start in the world: "No man is born rich. Every man, when he first sees light, is commanded to be content with milk and rags. Such is our beginning, and yet kingdoms are all too small for us! Farewell."[21]

Letter 23:
The Joys of the Philosophic Life

Seneca assures Lucilius he is not going to write to him about the weather or other trivial matters people turn to when they don't know what to say. No, he will write about the foundation, or rather the pinnacle, of a sound mind, which is not to find joy in useless things or to make our happiness dependent upon externals outside our control.[22] Indeed, he will exhort his dear friend to set it as his goal to learn how to experience the true joy that comes when one frees oneself from both the hope of external goods and the fear of things like poverty or death. "The very soul must be happy and confident, lifted above every circumstance."[23] This is the promise of philosophy, and it is fulfilled when one rejoices only in what comes from the best within oneself. And what is truly best? Real good "comes from a good conscience, from honourable purposes, from right actions, from contempt of the gifts of chance, from an even and calm way of living which treads but one path."[24] It is only a few who control themselves and their actions by a guiding purpose,[25] while the rest are swept along aimlessly by the river of life, some through sluggish waters and others in violent currents.

Seneca concludes with two related sayings of Epicurus that address the same theme that was addressed in Letter 13, that of the foolishness of perpetually getting ready to begin to live life rather than simply living it. Seneca says a man cannot be prepared to face death if he is just starting to live. We must strive rather to live as though we have already lived long enough by always living in harmony with our guiding purpose.

21. Ibid., 141.
22. Cf. Epictetus's *Handbook*, ch. 1.
23. *Epistles*, 161.
24. Ibid., 163.
25. Cf. Epictetus's doctrine of *prohairesis*.

Letter 31:
Goals Worth the Sweat

Seneca tells Lucilius that he recognizes him now! The old philosopher perceives from his young friend's correspondence that he is beginning to reveal in actuality the character that Seneca knew he possessed in potential. He sees that he is progressing in philosophy, striving for what it best and trampling under his feet the petty things of which the crowd approves. There is only one good, he reminds him; that cause and support of a happy life is to trust in oneself. This requires that one recognize that busyness, work, and toil are not true goods in and of themselves when they do not serve a noble purpose. One makes oneself happy through one's own efforts when those efforts are blended with virtue. Whatever is blended with virtue is good and whatever is joined to vice is evil. Good is the knowledge of things and evil is the lack of such knowledge.[26] When a good, noble goal has been identified, a good man will not fear the sweat involving in attaining it, even if it involves an arduous struggle uphill. The knowledge of good and evil in things human and divine will also lead to an even temperament and to a consistent, harmonious life.

And how is such a goal attained? Nature has provided you with all the necessary tools to rise to the level of God. Your money won't do that, since God has no property. Your fancy clothes won't do it either, for God has no wardrobe; nor will your fame and recognition, for no one truly knows God, and many do not honor him. Beauty and strength are useless here as well. They cannot hold up in old age. What we must seek is not things outside our control, governed by Fortune or Chance, but rather the goods of the human soul. "What else could you call such a soul than a god dwelling as a guest in the human body?"[27] Such a soul may dwell in a stately Roman knight, but just as well in a slave. Indeed, one may arise from the very slums and shape oneself into kinship with God. This

---

26. Cf. Epictetus's treatment of assent or dissent to impressions.
27. *Epistles,* 229.

likeness of God cannot be cast in gold or silver, but is molded within our souls.

Letter 39:
On Cultivating Greatness of Soul
(and the Dangers of Failing to Do So)

The most noble element within the human soul is its capacity to be roused to seek out honorable things. No man of great talents is pleased with things mean and petty. The vision of great things calls to him and inspires him. Our souls are like flames, always flickering in motion; and the more ardently a soul burns, the greater is its activity. Happy is the man whose soul burns for better things! This man will disregard the things of chance, control the level of his prosperity, diminish adversity, and despise the petty things that others admire. The great soul will scorn things commonly seen as great, and will prefer the ordinary when the ordinary is truly useful and the great is truly excessive.

Like a branch that is broken by too heavy a load of fruit is the soul that is ruined by unlimited prosperity and pleasure. Men who yield to excessive lusts always suffer in the end. They become unable to live without their vicious pleasures, so that what was once excessive and superfluous is now indispensable to them. They come to love their own vices. They attain the peak of unhappiness when they are not only drawn to but are pleased and contented by shameful things. At this point they become beyond cure, for their vices have become habitual.

Letter 53:
Philosophical Invincibility

Here Seneca provides another paean to philosophy, and an exhortation to pursue it above all else. Seneca begins his letter with a rather drawn-out account of a recent bout of seasickness he experienced on a journey. It had become so bad that when he persuaded the captain to come close to the shore, he jumped out into the cold waters in his woolly clothing and crawled over rocks onto the shore.[28] He quips that he concluded that Ulysses himself (Odysseus of Homer's *Odyssey*) kept getting stranded on islands not because of Neptune's (Poseidon's) ill will but because of his own seasickness! The moral of this little story was to show that while physical ailments have a tendency to make themselves known to us with unmistakable force and gusto, when it comes to ailments of the soul, the worse shape one's soul is in the *less* one is aware of it. He compares it to sleep. A person sleeping lightly may experience dreams and even realize that he is asleep and dreaming, while a person in heavy slumber has descended too deep for dreams or for consciousness of the self. A person who does not admit his spiritual failings is still stranded deep within them. A person can only remember his dreams when he wakes up, as recognizing one's faults is a sign of health. And what can wake a person up? Philosophy.

Only philosophy can rouse us from the slumbers that blind us to our faults. Seneca implores Lucilius to devote himself entirely to "her." If a sick person will devote his entire time to recovery before he carries out his normal business affairs, so too should we give precedence to the pursuit of wisdom and focus more on curing our souls than on any other business. Philosophy is a demanding mistress. She doesn't want only odd moments from us, but demands our attention full-time. Philosophy "tells all other occupations: 'It's not my intention to accept whatever time is left over from you; you shall have instead, what I reject.'"[29]

Seneca bids us give all of our time to philosophy, sit by her side and court her, giving her our own mind, and thus advancing ourselves beyond other men, "not far behind the gods themselves."[30] Indeed, Seneca declares that in a sense a wise man surpasses even a god, since a god is fearless by nature, while a wise man has earned his own fearlessness, achieving despite his human weakness the serenity of a god.

---

28. Part of Seneca's own regimen of physical training for health and mental toughness included bathing in frigid waters, much like modern "Iceberger" swim-clubs that take cold ocean dips on New Year's Day and on other wintry occasions.

29. *Letters,* 103.

30. Ibid.

Seneca ends with the lines that were used as this chapter's epigraph:

> Philosophy's power to blunt all the blows of circumstances is beyond belief. Never a single missile lodges in her; she has strong, impenetrable defenses; some blows she breaks the force of, parrying them with the slack of her gown as if they were trivial, others she flings off and hurls back at the sender.[31]

Letter 64:
The Grandeur of a Happy Life

Seneca tells Lucilius of a dinner party he had attended the night before. Those present stoked up the fire and conversed on one topic after another; and then someone read to them from a book by Quintus Sextius the Elder[32]: "Ye Gods, what strength and spirit one finds in him!"[33] Seneca notes that some philosophers parse words and quibble. They do not inspire the reader's spirit because they have no spirit. Sextius, however, was a great man and a real philosopher. He who reads Sextius will say:

> "He is alive; he is strong; he is free; he is more than a man; he fills me with a mighty confidence before I close his book." I shall acknowledge to you the state of mind I am in when I read his works: I want to challenge every hazard; I want to cry: "Why keep me waiting, Fortune? Enter the lists! Behold, I am ready for you!"[34]

Sextius inspires us to overcome obstacles, and shows us the grandeur of the happy life but without holding it beyond our reach. He shows it is something high, but attainable for those who have the will to seek it. Such is the effect of virtue itself. For Seneca himself, the contemplation of wisdom takes up much of his time as he gazes upon her, bewildered, just as he is when he gazes upon the starry

31. *Letters*, 103.
32. A Roman philosopher of the first century BC who combined elements of Pythagoreanism and Stoicism.
33. *Epistles*, 439.
34. Ibid.

sky and it strikes him as if he has just seen it for the first time. He worships the discoveries of wisdom and the great philosophers who discovered them. He delights in the inheritance they have provided us. They have laid up this treasure for us, but like good managers of a household they leave it to us to do our part to increase this inheritance. Much remains to be done, and much will still remain a thousand ages from now. Even if the ancient masters had discovered all there was to be discovered, there is always still a new task before us, to study and apply these advances made by our predecessors.

If a prescription had been handed down that healed all the maladies of the eye, we would not need to seek out a new another one, but to learn how to adapt it to the particular disease, and stage of disease, before us. The cures of the spirit were discovered long ago, but it is up to us to learn the methods and the right times to apply the treatments. We should also show respect, honor, and gratitude to those teachers who came before us, like Marcus Cato the Elder and the Younger, Laelius the Wise, Socrates and Plato, Zeno and Cleanthes. We should always rise to do honor to such noble names.

Seneca: From Lessons to Legacy

We've had but the smallest taste of the practical advice and wisdom of this great Roman moralist and man of the world. Readers are encouraged to dip directly into his letters and his essays, all of which are of historical interest and practical value. We'll examine a few more of the lessons from his letters in our legacy chapter, especially as we see how and why various Church Fathers and other later Christian thinkers found him such a kindred spirit—or held him in contempt.

9

A Legacy of Humanity the Whole Wide World Needs Now

Seneca was a Stoic, and Stoicism was the porch to Christianity. Then, as now, it was the thought-force that lay nearest to our inspirational religion.

⌒Richard Mott Gummere[1]

Nature bids me to do good to all mankind—whether slaves or free-men, freeborn or freed-men, whether the laws gave them freedom or a grant in the presence of friends—what difference does it make? Wher-ever there is a human being there is the opportunity for a kindness.

⌒Seneca[2]

We have had a glimpse of the "two Senecas." To some he was an opportunistic politician using philosophy to advance his own self-ish interests; to others a sincere lover of wisdom with serious human failings who yearned to more deeply practice what he preached, but whose earlier life choices in politics set him upon a narrow path with only one way out. From a Stoic perspective, we might say that by his youthful search for honors and influence, for things "outside our control" and at best indifferent to happiness, Seneca forged his own chains and gave a disturbed young emperor the key thereto. Those who read Seneca's works can form their own opinions of him as a man. Indeed, as we will see, no other Stoic has

---

1. *Seneca the Philosopher and His Modern Message*, 54.
2. "On the Happy Life" in *Seneca's Moral Essays, Volume II*, 163.

been subjected to such a mixed bag of criticism and praise over the centuries as has Seneca. This is compounded and multiplied by the fact that he that he has been panned or praised in his roles as tutor, administrator, tragedian, essayist, and scientist as well as moral philosopher.

We have seen in our relatively thorough treatment of the legacies of Musonius Rufus and Epictetus how the early Christians found so much in Roman Stoic morality that was worthwhile and kindred in spirit to their own faith; and how their legacies are waxing again in our time. The case has been much the same for the writings, if not the person, of Lucius Anneaus Seneca; so here I'll provide but a brief whirlwind tour of the particular legacy of this very human Stoic.

The Stoic Stylist in the Ancient Pagan World

Some of Seneca's earliest fame and notoriety came from his powerful impact as a public speaker in the Roman Senate. His popularity and the dazzling style of his orations prompted the envy and jealousy of the Emperor Caligula, who famously called Seneca's style of language "sand without lime,"[3] sizzle without substance, as we might say today.

The famous grammarian Quintilian, official head of the Roman schools of rhetoric, within a decade after Seneca's death would praise his writings for their wit; wealth of material; and noble sentiments in championing virtue against vice, which provide good material for building up one's character. However, he also warned young students of the many "ruinous elements" of Seneca's style, his tendency to indulge in "tricks" due to an undisciplined style born of too great a fondness for his own ideas. Indeed, Quintilian concludes (ending with a sentence reminiscent of Seneca's own elegant style and ear for catchy aphorisms) that "Our student should, however, pick and choose when reading Seneca, as I wish Seneca himself had done. For a nature that could get what it wished was worthy of wishing for better things."[4]

---

3. Both of which are needed to make cement—something solid!
4. Cited in Gummere, 35.

The powerful emperor Trajan (who reigned 98–117) applauded Seneca as an able administrator of the empire; while the grammarian Marcus Cornelius Fronto, friend and mentor to later Stoic Emperor Marcus Aurelius (who reigned 161–180), like Quintilian, took Seneca to task for "jog-trot sentences," "glaring patches," "sugar plums," and "easy lapses into slippery ways."[5] And yet Fronto also confesses that Seneca is still the most popular author among the young men of his day, many decades after Seneca's death. Seneca offered Stoicism with panache, a panache that not all, especially not all professional grammarians, found palatable. Still, his thoughts have been found most nourishing to countless seekers of wisdom who have taken the time to ingest and digest them.

Seneca: A Kindred Spirit in the Eyes of the Early Church

There were many real and imagined relationships between Seneca and the early Christian Church. We have noted that Seneca's brother Gallio appears in Acts 18:12–27, where he refuses to hear a case against St. Paul, a Roman citizen from Tarsus who would end his life in Rome. Some have speculated on the possibility that Seneca and Paul might have met, though there is no sound evidence of this. For a time there was a body of letters said to be a correspondence between the two men, but it has been found inauthentic. Still, there are indeed many ideas in Seneca's writings that parallel ideas found in Paul and in other books of the New Testament. It does not appear that Seneca took these ideas from Christian sources. The formal canon of the New Testament was not put together until more than 200 years after Seneca's death, and Seneca seems to have had little familiarity with the followers of Christ, who in Roman circles were often considered just another Jewish sect. Still, it is certainly possible that some Christian ideas in the air in the empire may have found their way to the ever-inquisitive Seneca.

Seneca's moral message was very well-received by some of the Church Fathers; Tertullian (160–220) calls Seneca "*saepe noster*,"

---

5. Ibid., 41.

"often ours," or almost a Christian. Seneca prepared the way for the acceptance of many ideas central to Christian morality, not only in his writings on the brotherhood of humanity and the dignity and worth of women and of slaves, but also through striking passages like these: "God is near you, he is with you, he is within you. This is what I mean, Lucilius: a holy spirit indwells within us, one who marks our good and bad deeds, and is our guardian."[6]

Medieval Scholastics Synthesize Seneca

The scientific works of Seneca were not unknown to great scientific minds like the Dominican friar St. Albert the Great (1200–1280) and the Franciscan friar Roger Bacon (1214–1294). Blessed Humbert of Romans (1200–1277), the fifth Master General of the Order of Friars Preachers, knew Seneca well as an orator and moralist. He cited him approvingly five times in his *Treatise on the Formation of Preachers*, a tome designed to guide the new Dominican Order in the most effective means to spread the gospel of Christ. Another Dominican theologian, Guillaume Peyraut (ca. 1200–1271), drew heavily from Saints Augustine and Bernard, but he also borrowed liberally from Seneca in his massive *Summary of Vices and Virtues*, which "treats of the seven deadly sins (gluttony, avarice, sloth, envy, vanity, anger) and the seven virtues (faith, hope, charity, temperance, fortitude, justice, and prudence) along with the eight beatitudes and the seven gifts of the Holy Spirit."[7]

In the theological writings of yet another learned Dominican, St. Thomas Aquinas, we see the highly careful analysis of Seneca's Stoic ethics that contributed to the magnificent synthesis of ethics found in the second of the three parts of Aquinas's monumental *Summa Theologica*. The *Summa's* first part focuses on God and Creation, and the third part on Christ and the Sacraments, while the second is devoted to the nature of man and his perfection through virtue. Seneca wrote in Latin, so he was directly accessible to St. Thomas,

6. Loeb, *Epistles 1–65*, 273.
7. Benedict M. Ashley, O.P., *The Dominicans* (Eugene, OR: Wipf and Stock, 1990), 31.

who was not fluent in Greek. Seneca and his ideas appear several times in the *Summa*, and I'll highlight just two of the important references.

We have seen that for Musonius Rufus, the four cardinal virtues of temperance, courage, justice, and prudence, played a central role, while Epictetus was far more inclined to speak of virtue in general. Seneca's writings address and analyze the cardinal virtues along with many others. This was a tradition found before him in Cicero and expounded upon twelve centuries later by Saints Albert and Thomas Aquinas. They would synthesize elaborate systems of virtues that included many other related virtues, which they classed according to different types.

The practical wisdom of prudence, for example, for Cicero and for St. Albert required three "integral parts" or faculties of memory, understanding, and foresight, for to obtain virtuous goals in the future (foresight) we must act intelligently in the present (understanding), guided by wisdom we've gleaned in the past (memory). By the time we come to St. Thomas, prudence has grown five additional integral parts: docility (teach-ability), shrewdness (capacity for quick judgment when necessary), reason (ability to apply universal principles to concrete, practical situations), caution (ability to restrain oneself from taking rash action), and circumspection (the habit of examining all of the particular circumstances that might impinge on the rightness of one's action). It is in St. Thomas's analysis and synthesis of the human psychology of virtue and vice that he calls upon Seneca's assistance.

In treating the virtue of *clemency*, St. Thomas classes it in its relationship to the virtue of *meekness*, an essential part of the virtue of *temperance*, because meekness tempers, controls, or regulates *the passion or emotion* of anger, while clemency moderates *external actions* of punishment that may arise from anger. Seneca wrote an entire composition *On Clemency*, hoping to instill some in Nero; and while Nero ignored it, St. Thomas read it carefully and used it extensively. He cites Seneca as his authority that "*clemency is leniency of a superior towards an inferior,*"[8] that "*clemency is a temperance of*

8. ST, II–II, Q. 157, a.1.

the soul in exercising the power of taking revenge," and in a smooth, silver-tongued Senecan statement that *"clemency is a certain smoothness of soul."*[9]

Seneca's own "smoothness of soul," mastery of language, and nobility of sentiment is seen most clearly in the way St. Thomas cites his authority in matters of the virtue of *gratitude*, an essential component of the virtue of *justice*, through which we render to another his rightful due. Seneca wrote no mere essay but an entire book on gratitude (*De Beneficis—On Benefits*). Here, St. Thomas intermingles time and again the thoughts of the Roman Stoic with the insights of Aristotle, Cicero, Scripture, and St. Augustine. Indeed, in his two questions of ten articles on gratitude and ingratitude (II–II, Qs. 106 and 107), St. Thomas cites Seneca more often than any of the others, in good thoughts and *bon mots* well worth cataloging for our own instruction:

- On whether one should discount a favor if it was easily performed: *"It is the height of malevolence to refuse to recognize a kindness, unless the giver has been the loser thereby."* (*De Benef.* vi)
- On how gratitude begins with a heartfelt attitude: "Hence Seneca says (*De Benef.* ii): *Who receives a favor gratefully has already begun to pay it back."*
- That we need not be rich to show gratitude: "Seneca writes (*De Benef.* vi): *There are many ways of repaying those who are well off, whatever we happen to owe them, as good advice, frequent fellowship, affable and pleasant conversation without flattery."*
- On how gratitude for a favor must be prompt, but repayment should not be hurried: "Seneca says (*De Benef.* iv): *He that hastens to repay, is animated with a sense, not of gratitude but of indebtedness."* Further, "Seneca says (*De Benef.* ii): *Do you wish to repay a favor? Receive it graciously."* Finally, "as Seneca observes (*De Benef.* iv), *he that wishes to repay too soon, is an unwilling debtor, and an unwilling debtor is ungrateful."*
- On the sinfulness of ingratitude: "Seneca declares (*De Benef.* iii) that *to forget a kindness is the height of ingratitude."* Thomas clarifies Seneca's intention to refer not to an unwillful failing of human memory, but to forgetfulness that comes from negligence: "For, as

9. Ibid., a.3.

Seneca observes (*De Benef.* iii), *when forgetfulness of favors lays hold of a man, he has apparently given little thought to their repayment.*"[10]

Note here as well a special affinity between the mindsets of Seneca and Aquinas in their intellectual magnanimity. Both men clearly and explicitly sought out, acknowledged, and promulgated truth, regardless of where it might be found. As we find in the works of St. Thomas not only citations to Scripture and Church Fathers, but countless citations of pagan philosophers, and Jewish and Muslim philosophers and theologians as well; so too we find in Seneca not only citations to earlier Stoics, but copious references to nuggets of wisdom found in other schools, from the garden of the Epicureans to the Academy of the Platonists. As he wrote to Lucilius: "The thought for to-day is one which I discovered in Epicurus; for I am wont to cross over even into the enemy's camp,—not as a deserter, but as a scout."[11]

In our modern time, when groups with opposing views are so prone to shout each other down, impugning their enemies' assumed motivations rather than grappling honestly with their ideas, this lesson of Seneca and St. Thomas Aquinas is truly one the whole wide world needs now. Indeed, it might make for fewer enemies.

Other prominent medieval writers made much ado of Seneca. Dante Alighieri quotes or closely parallels Seneca's language more than a dozen times in his writings. We find among the glorious pre-Christian spirits in the first circle of Dante's *Inferno* Greek and Roman thinkers and philosophers of the first rank: "With Orpheus, Zeno, and Hippocrates, Tullius, Linus, Seneca." In the works of Geoffrey Chaucer (1343–1400), the "Father of English Literature" explicitly cites Seneca and often parallels his thought.

10. St. Thomas's own last words on the vice of ingratitude are also worth noting here. In addressing the question "Whether Favors Should Be Withheld from the Ungrateful," he artfully employs Stoic and Christian medical metaphor in a most noble way: "He that bestows a favor must not at once act the part of a punisher of ingratitude, but rather that of a kindly physician, by healing the ingratitude with repeated favors."

11. Seneca, *Epistles* 1–65, Letter II, 9.

The Rebirth of Senecan Wisdom
from the Renaissance to Our Own Time

Moving toward our own time, the Renaissance thinker Petrarch (1370–1374) was an outspoken apologist for Seneca and his letters. Gummere even reports that in the late Middle Ages and early Renaissance the University of Piacenza in northern Italy had a Professor of Seneca. "This put him on a par with the study of Aristotle at the University of Paris."[12] The young humanist law-school graduate and later Protestant Reformer John Calvin (1509–1564) wrote his first published book on Seneca's *De Clementia*. He considered Seneca and Cicero two "ancient pillars," though he did criticize Seneca for some of his ideas and his style.

One of the greatest Christian promulgators of the Stoics in general and Seneca in particular was the philologist Justus Lipsius (1547–1606), whom we encountered briefly in chapters 4 and 6 through his praise for Epictetus. This Catholic revert from Lutheranism was a classical historical and literary scholar who published commentaries on the Roman historians Tacitus and Suetonius, as well as the Roman comic poet Plautus; but he was also an amateur lover of the wisdom that comes from philosophy. His book *De Constantia libri duo* ("*About Constancy* or *Concerning Constancy in two books*"), first published in 1584, has an intention very similar to this one in your hands, to inform and inspire Christian readers with the powerful wisdom of the ancient Roman Stoics. He does so in a very different style, though, in the form of a fictional dialogue between himself in his early thirties and a wiser, older, Seneca-like mentor by the name of Charles Langius.

On the blending of literature and philosophy, in the setting of Langius's beautiful garden at Liege (in modern Belgium) upon the riverfront of the Meuse, Langius advises young Lipsius not to become too attached to literature, but to build upon it with the weightier wisdom of the world of philosophy:

"If you sat down at a banquet, you would not, I believe, only have snacked of the dessert fruits and the cakes, but you would give

12. Gummere, *Seneca and His Modern Message*, 100.

your stomach the support of somewhat more substantial food. Why shouldn't it be the same in this public feast of learning? To the honey of the orators and poets, I say, why not join this solider food of Philosophy?"[13]

The main philosophical concept they discuss, is, of course, that of "constancy," which Lipsius defines as "*an upright and unmoved vigor of mind that is neither uplifted nor cast down by outward or chance appearances*"; and by "vigor" he means "a firmness deeply rooted in the mind, not by opinion, but by judgment and right reason."[14] Lipsius then develops themes most Epictetan and Senecan in two "books," the first with twenty-two and the second with twenty-seven chapters. He examines how to remain constant—modern editor/translator R. V. Young suggests "integrity" as a modern equivalent of constancy—and how to grow in virtue despite the ravages of public or private calamities.

Though he writes for Christians, his allusions are predominantly from the classical world. Indeed, R. V. Young's recent translation includes a new "To the Reader" section in a later addition written by Lipsius after the first edition of his book had come under some criticism from respected Christian readers who did not find it sufficiently Christian! He defends himself, stating that he wrote not as a theologian but as a philosopher; and that while Holy Scriptures contain higher truths, the truths of the philosophers are not therefore without worth. "I shall act as a philosopher, but a Christian philosopher," say Lipsius.[15] He concludes the new preface with these lofty thoughts:

> As the height of mountains is evident not at a distance, but when you have drawn near: likewise the splendor of philosophy is not apparent unless you learn it thoroughly. It cannot be thoroughly learned, however, without true Christian religion. If you take away this surpassing light—look, I acknowledge and proclaim: Philosophy is a mockery, a vanity, a madness. Tertullian said it well: "Who

13. Justus Lipsius's *Concerning Constancy*, ed. and trans. R. V. Young (Tempe, AZ: Arizona Center for Medieval and Renaissance Studies, 2011), 119.
14. Young, 28–29.
15. Ibid., 5.

knows truth without God, who God without Christ?" With this maxim I close and find peace in earnest. I should wish you to join me.[16]

Enough of Lipsius's *De Constantia* for now. It can still be read with pleasure and profit by Stoics and Christians in our day.

Seneca did not receive such approval from all Christian writers of Renaissance era, however. Capuchin Fr. Cajetan Mary da Bergamo (1660–1753), for example, warned his readers of Seneca's lack of humility: "Read the works of Seneca attentively—he who was held to exceed all philosophers in morality—and you will see how, in those very maxims with which he teaches magnanimity and fortitude, he also instills pride."[17] Fr. Cajetan wanted his readers to see God as the source of all virtues, and he believed Seneca encouraged man to pat himself on the back for the virtues that he may acquire. In his study on humility, he also wanted to focus on Jesus Christ as the fulfillment of all truth and the summit of morality. Nonetheless, even here we see acknowledgment of the praise historically bestowed upon Seneca's morality, and of the fact that people in Fr. Cajetan's day, more than 1,500 years after Seneca's death, Christians in Europe still read him.

Many other thinkers during these centuries studied Seneca's tragedies and scientific works as well as his moral essays and letters. In Seneca's tragedy *Medea*, for example, there is a verse that suggests the possibility of a new land across the Atlantic. Some thought this foretold the discovery of America; and indeed, Columbus himself was well aware of that passage.

Making that leap across to America and jumping ahead a few centuries, we find Seneca, like Epictetus, endorsed by Founding Fathers, including Thomas Jefferson. American poet Ralph Waldo Emerson (1803–1882) thought highly of Seneca as well, placing him

16. Ibid., 7. (Young noted that he could not track down that particular sentential in Tertullian's works, but cited a similar passage in his *Ad nations* 2.2, PL 588a. Perhaps I should not have been so harsh on the Internet in our Introduction, since a quick search yields these words of Tertullian in his *Treatise On the Soul*, chapter 1.)

17. Fr. Cajetan Mary da Bergamo, *Humility of the Heart*, trans. Herbert Cardinal Vaughan (Rockford, IL: TAN Books, 2006), 36.

in the highest of company: "Make your own Bible. Select and collect all the words and sentences that in all your reading have been to you like the blast of triumph out of Shakespeare, Seneca, Moses, John, and Paul."[18]

So where does Seneca's legacy stand today in our modern world? The ongoing interest in Seneca could not be more clear. As of today (January 25, 2015), for example, a search of "Lucius Anneaus Seneca" on a leading bookseller's website yields 3,201 hits under "Books," and 3,315 when expanded to "All Departments."[19] Seneca is of interest to this day to modern students of practical philosophy, to people seeking solace and self-improvement, to pastors and counselors who would hope to guide others to a more tranquil and fulfilling life. Perhaps he is most closely read and most explicitly promoted among modern societies devoted specifically to the rediscovery, application, and dissemination of the philosophy of the Stoics as guides to modern living. Hang on just a bit, though. I'll talk about these in our last legacy chapter on Marcus Aurelius (chapter 12), since he seems to hold a special place of honor in my own favorite group promoting Stoicism today.

18. Cited in Gummere, xvi.
19. And *this* book had yet to be published!

PART IV

Marcus Aurelius:
When Caesar Renders Unto God

✛

How can a mind find a sensible way to live? One way and one only—philosophy. And my philosophy means keeping that vital spark within you free from damage and degradation, using it to transcend pain and pleasure, doing everything with a purpose, avoiding lies and hypocrisy, not relying on another person's actions or failings. To accept everything that comes and everything that is given, as coming from that same spiritual source.

∼Marcus Aurelius (*Meditations, II.17*)[1]

---

1. Mark Forstater, *The Spiritual Teachings of Marcus Aurelius* (New York: Harper Collins Books, 2000), 203.

10

The Life of the Emperor
Who Bowed to the Slave

So blameless was the conduct of Marcus Aurelius that neither the malignity of contemporaries nor the spirit of posthumous scandal has succeeded in discovering any flaw in the extreme integrity of his life and principles.

~Rev. F. W. Farrar, D.D.[1]

SENECA, AS WE HAVE SEEN, counseled an emperor, and in the tumult surrounding an assassination plot on Nero, some thought perhaps he might become one—the first Stoic philosopher-king. Our last Stoic did indeed become a Roman Emperor, a living, breathing Stoic philosopher-king, the first and the last; and though he was undoubtedly aware of Seneca, we do not find Seneca mentioned in the philosopher-king's extant writings. As we will see in the next chapter, the philosophical emperor explicitly acknowledges his debt not to the Stoic near-emperor Seneca but to Epictetus, the Stoic ex-slave.

This "last Stoic," as he is sometimes called, Marcus Aurelius, ruled the world of the vast Roman Empire for 19 years; yet his most lasting contribution to mankind was a diary of sorts that he kept for himself, but which has provided strength, solace, and inspiration to countless souls in the nearly two millennia since he has been gone.

---

1. *Seekers After God: Seneca, Epictetus, and Marcus Aurelius* (Republished Classics, 2013)—originally published in 1868.

Let's proceed, then, to meet our last Stoic, this most noble "last Stoic," Emperor Marcus Aurelius.[2]

A Life of Training to Rule the World

On April 26, AD 121, the year of his second of three consulships of Rome for Marcus Annius Verus II, to his son Marcus Annius III and the latter's wife, Domitia Calvilla (a.k.a. Lucilla) was his grandson, Marcus Antoninus, born. The baby's father's side boasted descent from Numa, the second king of Rome, while his mother was also of ancient and noble lineage. Our Marcus was born during the reign of the third of the "five good emperors" under whom Rome stood at its peak of glory, influence, and prosperity. He was groomed by the third and the fourth to become the fifth and, unfortunately, the last.[3]

Marcus's father died when he was only around three years old, while his grandfather Verus, who helped raise him, would survive until Marcus's teens, and his mother would live until Marcus was about forty. Marcus sings the praises of both of them in his famous *Meditations*, the focus of our next chapter; and even his short-lived natural father is praised based on what he had heard of him as well as whatever he could remember. In the first three sentences of that timeless tome, he praised his grandfather for giving him a kind, even temper; his father for modesty and manliness; and his mother for his fear of God, generosity, not only abstention from evil but even the thought of it, and simplicity of life, untainted by luxury. If that was the case, they inculcated in Marcus the very traits for which he is so known and admired.

Though he would come to crave simplicity, he did grow up sur-rounded by wealth and luxury. His family lived on the Caelian hill of Rome, not far from the site where the impressive Basilica of St.

---

2. I will provide but the briefest of introductions. For those who would care to know Aurelius in much greater depth, I recommend Anthony Briley's comprehensive biography, fittingly entitled *Marcus Aurelius: A Biography* (New York: Barnes & Noble Books, 1999).

3. Emperor Nerva (reigned 96–98), Trajan (98–117), Hadrian (117–138), Antoninus Pius (138–161), and Marcus Aurelius (161–180).

John Lateran[4] now stands. The mature Marcus praises his grandfather for sparing him from a public education and providing him with the best tutors that money could buy, who would have begun to teach him at around the age of seven.[5] His spends most of the rest of the first book of his *Meditations* praising the various grammarians, mathematicians, musicians, trainers, and philosophers who not only fed him knowledge but helped shape the content of his noble character.

Marcus was known through his grandfather Verus to the emperor Hadrian, perhaps best known in our day for the great wall that bore his name defending the northern border of the Roman Empire in Britain. We will see that Marcus thought that one's eyes reveal one's character. Perhaps it was something in the child Marcus's eyes that captured the good will of the emperor, who nicknamed him "Verissimus," playing on his grandfather's name, which means "true," and amping it up to the max—"verissimus" meaning "truest." On February 25, 138, months before his death, Hadrian adopted Marcus's maternal uncle T. Aurelius Antoninus on the condition that Antoninus in turn adopt the 16-year-old Marcus (hence the name Aurelius), along with 7-year-old Lucius Commodus. Marcus was said to have been shocked at the adoption, but dreamt that night that his shoulders had turned to ivory and had been endowed with great strength. That July 8, the shoulders of Marcus's adoptive father would bear the weight of the world as Hadrian died, Antoninus succeeded him, and Marcus became co-heir to the empire.

Soon after, a previous betrothal for Marcus was canceled and he became betrothed to his cousin Faustina. She was but a child, several years younger than Marcus, and he would wait seven years until 145, when he was 24, to marry her. Within two years, she bore him a daughter, the first of many children.

4. The official basilica of the Pope as Bishop of Rome.
5. His informal education would have begun long before then, since it was a common practice for the wealthy Romans to employ Greek nursemaids for young infants to acquaint them with Greek, the preferred language of elegance and high culture for the Romans, and the language in which Marcus composed his *Meditations*.

Marcus took on various ascending ranks and positions within the world of Roman politics and state religion, including the penultimate rank of consul, which he held three times. During this time, his adoptive father Antoninus, long since also honored with the name of "Pius,"[6] had reigned with honor over the Roman empire. He died on March 7, 161, and Marcus become Imperator Caesar Marcus Aurelius Antoninus Augustus, co-emperor of Rome along with his younger adopted brother Lucius Commodus.

The two would reign in peace for nearly eight years, until the untimely death of Lucius at the age of 39 in 169. The 47-year-old Marcus would rule the world alone for eight years, until the time he elevated his own 15-year-old son Commodus as co-emperor at his side. The two would go forth together to successfully lead Roman legions against invaders threatening the empire from cold lands to the north. It was in various camps along the route of this expedition that Marcus would pen his immortal *Mediations.*

Marcus himself was of course as mortal as any other man, a fact that he often repeated to himself. On March 17, AD 180, not quite aged 59, Marcus died, possibly of plague, though some surmise that his son Commodus may have had a hand in his demise. In any event, that son of the philosopher would end the run of the five good emperors, bearing in some ways more resemblance to a Caligula or Nero than to his own father, the philosopher-king.

A Life of Training to Rule the Self

We've seen the brief highlights of the life of a man trained by others—and indeed by himself—to become a Roman emperor. But what makes this emperor so unique, so moving, so noble, and so inspiring, is that throughout his life he was far more interested in ruling his own inclinations toward passion, weakness, vice, and vainglory than he was in imposing his will upon others.

A timeline in Birley's biography of Marcus includes this notation: "146–7: Marcus turns wholeheartedly to philosophy."[7] We'll exam-

6. As was Aeneas, the pious, fabled founder of Rome in Virgil's first-century epic the *Aeneid.*

ine in our next chapter exactly what kind of philosophy this 25-year-old gave his heart to, a philosophy that would guide him until his last breath on earth. Birley is well aware that philosophy had long had a place in Marcus's heart and in his developing mind. Ancient writers described goals and behaviors of the 12-year-old Marcus that hark back to rugged ancient Cynics, and that presage not a few ancient and medieval ascetical Christian saints. He chose to wear the simple cloak of the philosophers and to sleep on the ground. Mothers will be mothers, of course, even in ancient Roman palaces; it was reported that only at his mother's insistence did young Marcus agree to sleep on a small bed covered with straw!

Marcus may have "played" philosophy as a child; yet he lived philosophy, not as a professional lecturer or teacher, but as a man who sought its wisdom to guide him in life; to become a good man; to master his desires and acquire the kind of virtues that could make him constant and calm as his shoulders of flesh, and not ivory, were called upon to bear the weight of the world. His philosophy, too, was hardly all about himself. He sought to be good so that he might follow God and serve with benevolence and kindness every person that he met and every person that God had placed under his earthly rule. Let's move on now to see how the king knelt before philosophy so that it might rule him.

---

7. *Marcus Aurelius: A Biography*, 44.

11

Lessons of Humble Grandeur

As surgeons always have their instruments and knives ready for cases which suddenly need their skill, so do you have principles ready for the understanding of things divine and human, for every act, even the smallest, remembering the bond which unites the divine and the human to one another. For neither will you do any human thing well without at the same time having regard to things divine, nor vice versa.

~Marcus Aurelius, *Meditations* II.13[1]

WE MOVE NOW to our last Stoic lessons, from the emperor who tried to cure his own soul and who can provide balm for our own souls today with his powerful healing medicine procured from the spiritual hospital that was the Stoic school. We have seen that the lessons of Rufus and Epictetus have come down to us in the second-hand form of alternately verbatim and condensed lecture notes. We emphasized Seneca's lessons from his famous *Letters*, essays within intended for the all the world in perpetuity in the form of personal correspondence. The primary lessons of Marcus Aurelius come to us in his *Meditations*, yet another genre, the most personal and intimate of all the Stoic writings.

In his early fifties and until his death, this gentle, benevolent man of ideas found himself year after year on the frozen banks of German rivers commanding the legions of Rome in defense of the

---

1. *Marcus Aurelius and His Times: The Transition from Paganism to Christianity*, trans. George Long (New York: Walter J. Black, 1945), 31.

world's greatest empire. But in the evenings, this reluctant man of war sheathed his sword and drew forth his pen, which has truly had mightier and farther-reaching results. At day's end he became a philosopher, to console his spirit; to cajole himself into virtue; and, whether he intended to or not, to provide similar consolation and inspiration to pagans and Christians alike for nearly two millennia.

The *Meditations* come down to us complete in twelve "books" (modern chapters) averaging about ten pages or so each in modern English translations. They appear to be the emperor's genuine personal thoughts, unintended for publication. Though Marcus undoubtedly knew of Seneca, and the two share a great number of Stoic sentiments, he does not mention Seneca by name in his works. Marcus wrote to himself in Greek, like Musonius Rufus and Epictetus; and as we will see, this mighty Emperor freely acknowledges the great influence the ex-slave Epictetus had on him.

The *Meditations* do not appear to be constructed in a systematic way, with the exception of the first autobiographical chapter serving as an introduction of sorts. They are not particularly polished, and similar themes come up again and again, though usually treated in somewhat different language or in a different context. They are notes to the self, representing Marcus's own written *askesis* or self-training in philosophy. Like our earlier Roman Stoics, Marcus is focused on practical *ethics,* how to apply philosophy to living the life a good person should live in accordance with nature. More unique to Marcus, perhaps, are his musings on the nature of nature, what was called *physics* by the Stoics then, akin to what we would call today *metaphysics,* the underpinnings of nature and why things are as they are. We see Marcus pondering the nature of the universe; whether there is a God or gods, and, if so, whether they intervene in the world; or whether everything is a really a matter of atoms, bouncing around by chance with no deeper meaning. He admits that such things are even hard for the Stoics to know for sure, but he has his opinion (in favor of God and purpose) and he advises living a life guided by philosophy regardless of the ultimate answer.

There are many hundreds of reflections in the *Meditations* (a total of 497 numbered sections or "chapters" in modern editions), from a sentence to a paragraph to a page or so each. I'd estimate

that it is probably around ten to twelve times the length of Epictetus's condensed *Handbook,* though significantly briefer than Epictetus's *Discourses* or Seneca's *Letters.* In presenting lessons from the
Meditations, I will have no choice but to be very selective, presenting just the smallest taste in hopes of whetting your appetite to feast
upon the *Meditations* themselves, whether for your first or your
one-hundredth time. In the sections that follow I will provide just a
few key ideas from each of the twelve books, striving to rarely
exceed one page. The text will be mostly paraphrase, guided by
three translations at my disposal, along with the ancient Greek text
as given in the Loeb Classical Library edition. The headings are
entirely of my own creation, each highlighting but one of the
themes I will emphasize.

Without further ado, then, let's find out what Caesar has rendered unto God as well as what insights he may render unto us.

Book I:
Gratitude 101

The first chapter of the *Meditations* consists of Aurelius's catalogue
of thanks to various family members and teachers who influenced
him, including one Sextus, grandson of the philosopher Plutarch,
from whom he learned "kindliness . . . and dignity without affecta-
tion; and an intuitive consideration of friends; and a toleration for
the unlearned and the unreasoning. And his tactful treatment of all
his friends, so that simply to be with him was more delightful than
any flattery. . . ."[2] From Alexander the Grammarian, Marcus learned
not to embarrass others by correcting their speech, but if possible to
later employ the correct pronunciation or usage in a statement of
one's own one to subtly provide the proper example. From Alexander the Platonist Marcus learned not to write "I am too busy" in
his letters or to use important business affairs as an excuse to evade
his normal obligations to those close to him. From his "father"
(adoptive father Emperor Antoninus Pius), this future emperor also

2. Marcus Aurelius, *Meditations*, trans. C. R. Haines (Cambridge, MA: Harvard
University Press, 2003), 7–9.

learned "a readiness to acknowledge without jealousy the claims of those who were endowed with any special gift, such as eloquence or knowledge of the law or ethics or any other subject...."[3] From the philosopher Rusticus, he learned that he needed to train and improve his character, to be forgiving, and to be careful in his opinions; and he gives him special thanks for supplying him with one particular book from his own library—the *Memoirs of Epictetus*.[4] Marcus also thanks the gods for such things as providing him with good ancestors, relatives, mentors, and friends; retaining his sexual purity for the proper time; keeping him from adultery; making him not so proficient in things like oratory, poetry, and logical studies, so that he might pursue philosophy as a guide for righteous living.

In the course of his catalog of thanks and praise, specific qualities and virtues Marcus acknowledges in various mentors include "sweetness of temper"[5]; modesty; manliness; generosity; abstention; simplicity; self-reliance; control of anger; "to possess great learning but make no parade of it"[6]; love of family, truth, and justice; optimism; confidence; stability; self-mastery; cheeriness; beneficence; mildness; unshakable steadfastness; love of work and the common good; sexual self-restraint; good humor; and foresightedness. That's quite a list for just his first chapter. Marcus truly had much for which to give thanks. But how do *we* acquire these things? Let's meditate for a moment on the next meditation as we allow Marcus to show us the way.

Book II:
On Achieving Equanimity

In Book II of the *Meditations*, Marcus Aurelius begins with a paragraph of advice that we might all do well to read first thing every day, right after morning prayers! The kindly emperor tells us that upon arising each day we should say to ourselves that we are going

---

3. Ibid., 17 (a trait none-too-common among Roman emperors).
4. Most likely the *Discourses*.
5. Ibid., 3.
6. Ibid., 9.

to encounter "the busybody, the thankless, the overbearing, the treacherous, the envious, the unneighborly"[7]; and though more than two-thirds of a million days have passed since he wrote those words, I think they still ring true for us today (and tomorrow). He goes on to say that we should remind ourselves that such people act this way because they do not truly understand the beauty of goodness and the ugliness of evil; that we cannot truly be debased or injured by them if we *do* understand the good; that they share with us the same humanity and capacity for reason; and that we cannot hate them, but must value them as kinsmen, placed in the world for cooperation, and not for resentment and aversion. Whew!

In other words, he tells us that we can remain calm in our minds and loving in our hearts if we forgive one another our faults—in advance! If I may call to mind Dr. Ellis's ABC scheme from chapter 6, inspired by the Stoics after all, the emperor would have us plant rational beliefs in our mind ahead of time, ready to spring forth to counter life's little unfortunate events that are simply bound to happen.

That Marcus took this project seriously there is not the slightest doubt. The middle-aged ruler of an empire chides himself as an "old man" who needs to stop acting like a slave or a puppet pulled about by impulses. He even admonishes himself for his thirst for books, so that he should not die "murmuring"—mumbling to himself from such excessive reading that his soul cannot rest and he cannot die in peace. He affirms his desire to put his philosophical learning into daily practice every day, never complaining of his lot or fretting about what the future may hold.

He warns as well against five ways in which the soul harms itself:

1) By grumbling about anything that happens to us, which is to rebel against nature.
2) By turning away from or opposing any person with the intent to cause harm, as we do when angry.
3) By being overcome by either pleasure or pain.
4) By wearing a mask and acting or speaking insincerely or untruthfully.

7. Ibid., 27.

5) By acting aimlessly, wasting time and energy on things that do not serve the end of rational beings—to follow reason and the laws of one's city and of the universe.

Book III:
On the Beauty of the Universe Outside and In

Marcus begins with the sobering thought that with each day our life is waning away. We know not how much time remains and whether or not we might lose our mental faculties, even while still alive. For this reason we must make haste to try to better grasp the nature of the universe and to make ourselves useful to others, while we still have the capacity to do so.

Since an underlying tone of a sad melancholy and tired resignation is sometimes observed in Marcus's *Meditations*, his next observation may represent a surprising paean to the simple pleasures and joys ever available to the thoughtful Stoic. In a passage that might call to mind a popular song of the 1970s, Ray Stevens's *Everything is Beautiful*, Marcus argues essentially just that! Even the smallest things that come about by nature bear a certain beauty and attractiveness to us, from the cracks that open in bread while it bakes, to the gaping of ripe figs and olives, to bending ears of corn, to the eyebrows of a lion, indeed, all the way to the foam that flows right from the mouth of the wild boar! While we might not perceive all beauty with a superficial glance, a person who has learned to be at home with nature and her works will see pleasing beauty everywhere, in the actual gaping jaws of wild beasts as much as in their portrayals in sculpture, in the ripeness and comeliness of older persons of both sexes, and in the chaste but alluring loveliness of the young.

We should seek such beauty in our souls as well. We should train ourselves and discipline our thoughts, so that at any time, if someone were to ask us, "What were you just thinking about?," we might answer immediately and truly, so that it is clear that our thoughts are sincere and kindly, dwelling on what befits a rational, social animal, that cares not for sensual pleasures, rivalry, envy, suspicion, or anything else that would make us blush, were we to admit it.

Book IV:
The Primacy of Perspective

Here Marcus reminds himself of the power of perspective, from many different perspectives! He notes how wealthy men build houses of retreat for themselves in the country, on seashores, or on mountains; but the surest retreat to restore one's calm and freedom is the retreat to within one's own soul. Within one's soul should reside short and sweet principles that will bring inner peace. If you are disturbed by the wickedness of others, remind yourself that they know not what they do and that forbearance is part of the virtue of justice. How many men who have fought and quarreled now lie dead, reduced to ashes? If you are disturbed by your lack of fame and acclaim, consider how quickly all is forgotten. The whole earth is but a tiny point in the universe, and how vast—endless—is the time on either side of the present.

Here are two maxims to keep close at hand. First, remember that things outside us cannot disturb our souls by themselves, but only through our wrong opinions.[8] Secondly, remember that everything that you see is in the process of changing and soon will be no more. The universe is change, and life is a series of impressions.

Here are two more key maxims. First, do only what your powers of reason determine is for the good of mankind. Secondly, change your opinion about what you should do if someone proves to you that you are wrong.

See human life from the perspective of time. In the days of Vespasian, people hurried about marrying, raising children, getting sick and dying, coveting things and honors. They are all dead and gone. Move to the time of Trajan, and again all is the same; and the same applies to any epoch of other times or nations: they are all gone without a trace. We must remember this lesson and not pursue vanities, as we have time only for this: to have just thoughts, social acts, honest words, and a disposition that gladly welcomes whatever happens.

Marcus chides himself: he will soon be dead and is not yet free

---

8. Extremely Epictetan, no?

and simple, fearing no external thing, treating all with kindness, and seeing that justice and wisdom are one.

Book V:
Rising to the Work of a Human Being

Have you ever had a hard time getting up in the morning? Marcus knew what that was like, perhaps especially when guarding frozen rivers with hordes of armed enemies on the other side. In any case, Marcus offers this advice: say to yourself, "I am rising to do the work of a human being. Why then am I dissatisfied if I am about to do the things for which I was brought into the world? Or was I made to lie under bedclothes and keep myself warm?"[9]

In a call to humility and duty, the emperor exhorts himself to deem no word or deed beneath him that is in accord with nature, regardless of what others might say. Let others follow their own guiding reason—each person must follow his or her own.

When you do a good deed for someone else, he tells us, don't be like people who consider that person their debtor; rather, be like the vine that produces its grape and having done so asks nothing more. When you do a good deed, don't proclaim it abroad, but get out there and do another.

Cherish what is best in the universe, that which directs and controls all things. Cherish as well the best thing inside you, because this is like the other. Your mind is the ruling faculty by which your own life is directed.

Ask yourself how you have treated the gods, your parents, siblings, wife, children, teachers, tutors, friends, relations, and household. Can you truly say of yourself this line from Homer: "*Never has he wronged a man in word or deed*"?[10]

How soon you will become ashes or a set of dry bones! Why, then, wait to do your duty, to honor the gods and bless them, doing good to men, with patience and forbearance, remembering all the

9. Long, 45.
10. *Odyssey* IV.690, as cited in Long, 54.

while that what happens to your poor breath and flesh neither belongs to your nor is under your control?

Book VI:
Turn Not into a Caesar!

Marcus was literally "turned into a Caesar," the second of all Roman ranks under that of Augustus, when Antoninus Pius raised declared him so in the year 140. Upon Pius's death, the ultimate title of Augustus would become Marcus's as well. So why does the emperor tell himself not to turn into a Caesar, not to become "Caesarified," in a more literal translation of his own Greek?

Well, we saw with Caligula and with Nero the kind of monster some Caesars became, even under the tutelage of a Stoic of the caliber of Seneca! They bristled at the slightest insult, real or imagined; simmered in envy at anyone else's excellence, and thought nothing of slaughtering any friend, family member, or foe who got in their way. Who was more un-philosophical, more disturbed and deranged by people and things outside of their own moral purpose? Marcus sought to avoid this at all costs.

He reminds himself that he thinks nothing of it if a man should scratch him or hit him in the course of gymnastic exercises in the ring. He does not hold that man in suspicion or mark him for retribution. He reminds himself to act that way in all areas of life, shrugging off the minor insults of those who seem to injure him.

When he urges himself not to become a Caesar, he notes how the position has warped men before and could do so again.[11] To avoid this fate, he exhorts himself to stay simple and good, to worship the gods, to show others affection, to advance in philosophy, and never to neglect the duties of a man: "Reverence the gods, and help men. Life is short. There is only one fruit of this earthly life, a pious disposition and social acts."[12]

---

11. And little did he know that his own son Commodus would one day become "Caesarized" like one of their ilk.

12. Long, 61.

In an earlier meditation, he notes how Alexander of Macedon (a.k.a. "the Great") and his horse's groom both shared the same fate; for they were either taken back into the creative principle of the universe or scattered upon the atoms. Rulers of men are no exception. Marcus uses his stepfather Antoninus Pius as an example of an emperor who did not turn into a Caesar, but rather was consistently rational, thoughtful, pious, sweet, unsuspicious, tolerant of free speech, grateful to those who could teach him something, straightforward in all his dealings with men, and religious without superstition.

Book VII:
Love Mankind. Follow God.

Among the many lessons here, Marcus counsels himself not to fear the future but face it with the same reason he now uses to face present things. He ponders next the intricate interweaving of all things in the universe, everything intertwined and held with a sacred bond. Though the universe holds countless things, they have all been arranged and combined to produce one ordered universe. The one universe is made up of everything, and there is one God who pervades all things, one substance, one law, one reason common to all intelligent creatures, and one truth. All rational beings are perfected by living in accordance with nature and reason. As it is with the various members of a unified body, although rational beings exist separately they are made for co-operation. Repeat to yourself, therefore, "I am a limb of the organized body of rational things."[13] If you see yourself only as a separate part, you do not love mankind in your heart, and doing good does not delight you for its own sake. When you see yourself as an essential member of a unified system of humanity, then you will see that the good you do for others also does good unto you.

We play our essential role when we subdue our imaginations, check our impulses, pay attention to what others say to us, clothe ourselves with modesty and simplicity, practice indifference toward

13. Haines, 169.

things outside of virtue and vice, observe the paths of the stars to remove our focus from lowly things of the earth, consider earthly things as if viewed from a perch high above, accept our present circumstances, act justly toward others, and control our thoughts so that nothing unexamined should steal into them. To put it in a nutshell: "Love mankind. Follow God."[14]

Book VIII:
Throwing Away Bitter Pickles

Marcus starts with a tip to himself on how to avoid vainglory: recall how clear it is to himself and to others that he has not lived his whole life as a philosopher, and that indeed he is far from philosophy now. Admit the truth and don't care what others think of you, but continue to relentlessly pursue a life in accordance with nature. This is done by sticking to one's principles. Which principles? Those that treat of good and evil, holding that there is nothing good for a man that does not make him just, temperate, manly, and free; and that there is nothing bad that does not make him the opposite.

Before you undertake any action, ask yourself, "How does this affect me?" "Will I come to regret it?" Soon you will be dead and all external things will be gone. What more should you seek, then, than to do the work of a rational and social being under the one law of God?

So where do the bitter pickles come in? If you come across a bitter pickle, by all means toss it away; and when your path is blocked by thorns go another way. That's all there should be to it. When you ask, "Why are such things even put in this world?," then you have gone too far and shown your ignorance of the workings of nature. You'd be laughed at by a carpenter or a cobbler if you complained that there was sawdust or parings accumulating on the floor from the things they are making. They have a place to dispose of such shavings and cuttings. Nature has no place outside of herself, and yet so wondrous is her craftsmanship that every bit of apparent

14. Long, 73.

refuse is absorbed and recycled to bring forth other new things. When you understand nature you will marvel at it, not complain about it.

Book IX:
On Contentment from Womb to Tomb

Injustice toward men is impiety towards the highest divinity, because the universal nature has made rational beings for the sake of one another, to help one another for mutual benefit, and by no means to cause harm. Lying is also impiety, because this universal nature is also named truth, and is the primary cause of all things that are true. To pursue pleasure as a good and to flee from pain as an evil is impiety too, for it implies that nature doles out goods to men unfairly.

How grand to end one's life without having tasted lying and hypocrisy and luxury and arrogance—but the next best thing is to take one's last breath when one has had quite enough of such things. We should not fear death, but rather recognize it as a most natural process and welcome it when it comes to us. This is a key to contentment, to recognize the natural stages of life: "As you now wait for the time when the child shall come out of your wife's womb, so be ready for the time when your soul shall fall out of its envelope."[15]

Cessation from activity is not an evil, and neither is death. Consider the seasons of your own life from childhood and youth to adulthood and old age. Each change was a kind of death for the stage that came before it, and yet it was nothing to fear. Soon the earth will cover us all, and then the earth itself will change, as will all that results from those changes. Indeed, loss is nothing but change, and the universal nature delights in change.

Do not be disturbed and complain about these facts, but strive to make yourself more simple and more worthy before the gods. If you pray to them, don't pray that things will or won't happen, but that

15. Long, 93.

you will be delivered from fear or desire or pain, regardless of what should happen. One man prays to lie with a certain woman when he should pray to be free of desire for her. Another man prays to get rid of an enemy, when he should pray to not wish to be rid of him. A third man prays that he should not lose his child, when he should pray that he should not dread the child's loss. Try praying like this, and then see what comes of it.

Book X:
Don't Talk About the Good Man—Be One!

Marcus begins this book by chiding himself, wondering if his soul will never be good and simple, at one with itself and "naked," more clear and visible than the body that holds it. He asks himself if he will never enjoy a loving and contented disposition. Later, he chides himself for talking about what a good man should be and not instead simply *being one*.

How does he work to accomplish this? He reminds himself again of important things to always bear in mind: that he is a part of a greater whole with an assigned part to play; that nature has equipped him to bear anything that comes his way with his power to shape his own opinion of things; that he is to try to instruct those who do harm, and if he is unsuccessful, neither to blame them or himself; that he is to strive after goodness, modesty, truth, wisdom, sympathy, and magnanimity.

The key to the greatness of soul that is magnanimity is to constantly study how everything changes and to be aware that one's own time is fleeting, that what others think about one does not matter, but only living contentedly and acting justly, dropping all unnecessary cares and endeavors, desiring nothing but to run the straight course through the law of nature, and thereby following God. When we remember that we are like leaves that will soon fall to the ground, that our children are too, that those who mourn our death with soon in turn be mourned, we will remember our true nature and our need to follow God in the present, the only time that is truly ours.

Book XI:
So Honest and Good You Can Smell It!

Marcus reviews the inward-looking and outward-acting properties of the rational soul. Unlike the souls of plants or animals, the human soul sees itself, analyses itself, shapes itself to its own will, and enjoys its own fruits. It extends itself out into the universe and all throughout the infinity of time, seeing that everything comes and goes and comes back again. By the time a man is forty, he should be aware of the sameness of what has come and what will come. There are other important properties of the rational soul: to love one's neighbor, the truth, and modesty; and to prize nothing above the things of the soul.

A man who truly prizes the goods of the soul, who is simple and good, should be like the man who has a strong smell, so that any who come near him must smell him, whether they want to or not! Hyperbole aside, the good character and good will of a man should show clearly through the look in his eyes.

In this book the ruler also gives himself nine rules to remember, as if a gift from the Muses, to reflect upon whenever someone has offended him.

1) Men were made for one another in mutual interdependence, as the ram for the flock and the flock for the ram, the ruler for the ruled and the ruled for the ruler.
2) Men act as they do according to the convictions they have acquired. They are self-made slaves to the opinions and principles they hold, and what they do makes sense to them.
3) Therefore, if they act rightly we should not be disturbed, and if they act wrongly neither should we be disturbed, since they acted out of their error and ignorance.
4) Remember your own faults too, and the fact that when you do abstain from wrongful acts it is often because of fear of your reputation, and not because you have conquered the inclination toward sin.
5) Don't be quick to judge, because you so often do not know if men have truly done wrong or not, since you don't know all of the circumstances surrounding their actions.

6) When you are angry at someone, remember that our life is but a moment, and soon we will all be laid out in death.

7) It is not truly the acts of others that disturb us, since these arise from *their* ruling principles, but rather our opinions about them.[16]

8) Consider how much more we suffer from our own anger than from the actions that prompt it.

9) Genuine benevolence is invincible. Correct another man with gentle kindness, without lecturing him or putting him on the spot, showing him that we are not made by nature to try to harm one another, and that when he strives to harm another he is only harming himself.

Marcus reminds himself as well to avoid not only anger, but also pandering and flattery. Both are against man's nature. The more a man controls his passions, the freer a man he is. Self-control is strength. Surrender to passion is weakness.

Marcus offers a tenth rule as one given by Apollo himself, the leader of the Muses: to expect bad men not to act badly is madness. Don't expect the impossible. Furthermore, don't expect that if you do not try to correct their evil they will not act wrongly towards you as well.

I will end with one last brief and simple meditation. Marcus points out that at their outdoor spectacles, the Lacedaemonians[17] saved seats in the shade for strangers, but they themselves sat wherever an open seat might be found. What a touching, gracious thought for the ruler of the world to endorse!

Book XII:
Fear Not Death, but Failure to Live

We come to the last of Aurelius's twelve books and here will highlight but a few thoughts that we might take to heart. In a previous

---

16. Note the affinity with one of Epictetus's foundational principles in chapter 5 of the *Handbook*, and, as we saw, with the keynote of modern cognitive psychotherapy.

17. The famously simple and rugged Spartans.

meditation,[18] Marcus notes that life is more like a wrestling match than a dance—we have to expect to face obstacles. Here Marcus again employs combative metaphors, telling us that in employing our philosophical principles we are to live not like the gladiator but like the pancrationist[19]; for while the gladiator is killed if he drops his sword, the pancrationist is always armed with his own two hands. We must never forget that God has given to us in our ruling reason all the power we need to do what he bids us and to accept whatever he gives us. If something is not right, don't do it. If something is not true, don't say it. Always keep social purposes in mind and always direct your acts to social ends.

What an honor to be a citizen of the world. Do not complain how long your citizenship lasts, and be aware it could end at any time. Imagine a director calling an actor away from a stage:

> "But I have not finished five acts, but only three of them." Good, but in life the three acts are the whole drama. For what shall constitute a complete drama is determined by him who first caused its composition, and now its dissolution; but you are the cause of neither. Depart then serenely, for he who releases you is also serene.[20]

So ends Marcus's *Meditations*. Let's move on to see what the world has made of the emperor's noble ideas in the 1,800 years since he left life's stage.

---

18. VII.61.

19. As noted in a previous chapter on Epictetus, men akin to our modern mixed martial artists, who combined boxing and wrestling but employed no weapons.

20. Marcus Aurelius, *Meditations*, in *Marcus Aurelius and His Times: The Transition from Paganism to Christianity* (Roslyn, NY: Walter J. Black, Inc., 1945), 133.

12

A Legacy of Nobility
to Inspire the Same in Us

Marcus Aurelius is the conspicuous example of the tendency to those modes of thinking, feeling, and living, which brought heathenism as near as in its own strength and wisdom it could come to Christianity.
⌒James Baldwin Brown[1]

It's in the nature of books about the spirit that they can be visited again and again. How often we return to books after a gap of some years and find that, with broader experience, we are able to read them in a deeper way, to see new facets that we had previously missed. Marcus Aurelius's book is one of these—it can't be outgrown; it does not date. It reads in a different way to someone who is twenty than to someone who is sixty yet still has something profound to tell them both about living the real good life.
⌒Mark Forstater[2]

THOUGH MARCUS WROTE them as self-training exercises, encouraging and sometimes chastising himself to live the life of Stoic virtue, countless people throughout the ages have found the *Meditations* full of moving insights that have spoken to their souls too. His legacy is vast and enduring. Here we'll briefly sample some of its highlights and lowlights, in hopes that they might prove enlightening.

---

1. James Baldwin Brown, *Stoics and Saints* (Glasgow: James MacLehose and Sons, 1893), 56.
2. Mark Forstater, *The Spiritual Teachings of Marcus Aurelius*, 12.

In This Corner, Marcus
Aurelius; and in This Corner, Jesus Christ?

Our thesis is that the Porch in some ways helped prepare ancient souls for the way of the Cross. Further, as is seen in this chapter's epigraph from a 19th-century British Congregational minister, philosophically learned Christians have noted that in some respects Marcus came as close to the Cross as any pagan writer. How ironic, then, that he is the only of our four great Roman Stoics to have actually persecuted Christians, or at least to have allowed for persecution. Consider the lifespan of the great early Christian Father St. Justin Martyr, for example (AD 100–165), and you will note that he died during Marcus's reign. His trial, conviction, and beheading happened under the auspices of the prefect Junius Rusticus in the city of Rome itself. To make matters more regrettable, Justin was also a philosopher who had written to Marcus's adoptive father Antoninus attempting to explain the faith. He acknowledged the pearls of wisdom of Greek philosophy as "seeds of Christianity," and considered great icons of the Stoics such as Plato and Socrates to be essentially unknowing, practicing Christians.

The execution of Justin seems entirely inconsistent with Marcus's philosophy of tolerance and love for mankind, and is probably best explained by Marcus's lack of factual knowledge about the true nature of Christ and Christianity. He clearly references Christians only once in his *Meditations.* In Book XI, chapter 3, Aurelius pines for a soul that is willing to be separated from the body at any time, whether that means the soul is to be demolished or dispersed or to continue to exist. He says this fearless willingness most come, however, from a person's own reasoned judgment, and not from mere "obstinacy" or "opposition," as he believed was the case for Christians.[3] Marcus clearly saw Christianity as a religion opposed to reason rather than one in which reason and faith might exist in harmony. (One can only imagine the emperor's opinion of Christianity's reasonableness had he lived in the days of St. Thomas

---

3. This echoes, to some extent, Epictetus's reference to the "Galileans" in the same context in *Discourses* IV.7, as we mentioned in chapter 6.

Aquinas.) Marcus also saw the Christians' refusal to sacrifice to the old Roman gods as evidence of traitorous intentions toward the Roman Empire, to defend which was his chief duty.

In any event, we are unable to know in any real depth Marcus's own heart and mind in regards to the Christians in his time, let alone his thoughts on the fullness of Christian belief—the full canon of the New Testament would not even be established until more than 100 years after Marcus's death. Our time and energy will be much better spent in tracing that which in Marcus is consistent and noble, as valuable today as it was in the second century.

The Death and Resurrection of Marcus's *Meditations*[4]

We do not know exactly how Marcus's *Meditations* were at first pre-served—possibly by his son-in-law Pompeianus or his close friend Victorinus. Some early writers seem to make indirect references to the work, but the first direct mention comes 170 years after Marcus's death in an oration of the philosopher Themistius.

After approximately 550 years of silence, around the year 900 we find some thirty quotations from the *Meditations* in the compilation of Suidas,[5] who mentions that it contains twelve books. A bishop of Cappadocia, Arethas, apparently owned a copy of the *Meditations* and mentioned it thrice in his writings.

About another 250 years pass and we find passages from books IV and V, attributed to Marcus, in the writings of Tzetzes a grammarian from Constantinople.

Moving ahead another 150 years brings us to around AD 1300 and a mention of the *Meditations* in the writings of the Christian Church-historian Nicephorus Callistus.

The first English edition appeared in London in 1634, translated by one Meric Casaubon. Another widely-circulated edition, often panned by critics for its "coarseness" or even "ludicrous expres-

---

4. This section summarizes primarily the history provided in Haines's Loeb translation of the *Meditations*.

5. The same man who, as we saw in Chapter 6, had cited Epictetus as well.

sions," appeared in London in 1747, translated by Jeremy Collier. Yet this translation would go on to be praised by the 19ᵗʰ-century English poet Matthew Arnold, who insisted that special honor was due to a man who introduced so many people to a man like Marcus Aurelius, whose acquaintance brings such "imperishable benefit."

We have seen how the *Meditations* appeared again and again in new translations in London. They also quickly made their way across the Atlantic, to be found in the libraries of American Founding Fathers, including John Adams and Thomas Jefferson.

A great many other English translations would appear throughout the years, and I'll quickly mention two more, since they are the two through which I have received the "imperishable benefit" of coming to know the thoughts of Marcus Aurelius. I have cited from the George Long translation, originally published in London in 1862. It is the translation that appears in the 1945 Modern Library edition (and one that I picked up for a dollar at one of our library's yearly used-book sales—a dollar well spent, indeed). A second is the translation by C. R. Haines, first published in 1916 by Harvard University Press as a part of their Loeb Classical Library (which includes the original Greek on facing pages).

The Most Statuesque of the Stoics

Recall from our discussion in chapter 7 the very different ways in which Seneca was represented in two very different busts—from the lean, grizzled, bearded "pseudo-Seneca" to the softer, rounder, balder, and likely more realistic double-headed bust depicting Seneca on one side and Socrates on the other. Despite the interesting story of the "two Senecas," Marcus, one could argue, was the most "statuesque" of all the Stoics. There is a famous equestrian statue of a dignified Aurelius astride a horse, bearded, without weapons, his right arm raised in a gesture of clemency. The magnificent larger-than-life bronze statue stands 14 feet tall and has quite an interesting history of its own. Though it is not mentioned in ancient sources, it was most likely erected in Rome in during Marcus's lifetime to celebrate victories over German tribes in AD 176. It was one of twenty-two "*equi magni*," gigantic equestrian statues erected in

Rome around that time. Many imperial statues were later melted down; this is the only one to survive to our day.

It apparently stood in the Lateran section of Rome (not far from Marcus's family home and the current Basilica of St. John Lateran) as early as the late eighth century, inspiring the emperor Charlemagne to seek out something similar for his palace in Aachen. In 1538 Pope Paul II ordered the statue transferred to the Capitoline Hill. It was to be refurbished by no less a sculptor than Michelangelo. Today the statue can be seen in the Capitoline Museum, and there is a replica in the Capitoline square.[6]

The Emperor Returns in the Most Surprising Places

• Several years back, while reading the diaries of Elisabeth Leseur (1866–1914), pages so poignant and powerful that after her death her atheistic husband was led to the Church and to the priesthood, I came across some lines on reason, duty, meditation, and examination of conscience that made me think, "Hey, she knew the Stoics!" On the very next page, there was the name of Marcus Aurelius![7]

• P.G. Wodehouse's (1871–1975) fictional genius and gentleman's gentleman *Jeeves* is most fond of quoting Aurelius.

• John Adams and Thomas Jefferson were not the only U.S. Presidents fond of Marcus Aurelius. In 1992, aides reported that the *Meditations* were among the favorite reads (and re-reads) of then President-elect Bill Clinton.

• Have you seen the movie *Gladiator* (2000)? If so, then you've seen Marcus Aurelius as portrayed by Richard Harris.

• Monty Python, Marcus Aurelius, and the Holy Grail? Also in the year 2000, Mark Forstater, the movie and television producer best known for the 1975 hit comedy spoof *Monty Python and the Holy Grail* came out with the book *The Spiritual Teachings of Marcus Aurelius*, so powerfully had the *Meditations* influenced his life.

---

6. A much smaller version can also be seen on the back of the modern half-Euro coin.

7. Elisabeth Leseur, *Light in the Darkness: How to Bring Christ to the Souls You Meet Each Day* (Manchester, NH: Sophia Institute Press, 1998), 44.

• Lastly, and perhaps coming to a venue near you, have you happened to catch Emperor Marcus Aurelius's stand-up comedy routine? Well, actually the Stoic Australian comedian Michael Connell, toga-clad and all, portraying Aurelius in a skit on Stoic comedy, of all things. *"Hey, you know what annoys me?—Nothin'. . . . Airplane food, now that's something I can endure!"*[8]

Marcus Aurelius and Stoicism Today

It was after I came up with the idea for this book that I discovered that Marcus Aurelius and his Stoic spiritual brethren are very alive and well on a blog and a corresponding movement called "Stoicism Today." From the fact that a seated representation of Marcus Aurelius writing his *Meditations* adorns the Stoicism Today website's home page and the cover of their first book is adorned with a bust of the emperor, it appears that they have a special affinity for the ideas of Marcus Aurelius, along with Epictetus and Seneca, the two other major Roman Stoics whose works exist in more than fragments.

Stoicism Today started in a workshop at the University of Exeter in the United Kingdom in October 2012 and has grown in size and scope every year since. Each November they host a "Stoic Week" featuring lectures and interactions with some of the world's greatest authorities on Stoicism and on modern cognitive psychotherapies. They promote the practical value of Stoic ideas through their thriving blog (http://blogs.exeter.ac.uk/stoicismtoday), managed by Ph.D. student Patrick Ussher, who is an expert on Stoicism, particularly in its relation to "Western Buddhism" and on Stoicism's broad applicability to the challenges of modern life.

Their group conducts seminars, produces and links downloadable videos, and has recently published a book entitled *Stoicism Today: Selected Writings* (Volume 1).[9] With contributions from multiple authors of varying backgrounds, the book offers practical wis-

8. (And what delivery, too! See michaelconnel.com.au. and check out his clips on YouTube or on the Stoicism Today website.)

9. I assume and hope from the "Volume 1" that additional volumes must be on the way.

dom from and for everyone from professional philosophers, to psychotherapists, to individuals facing disabilities, imprisonment, and other hardships, to people trying to be better parents, employees, employers, and citizens. Some of the group's most dedicated and prolific proponents have written and spoken about the transformative effects that Stoic philosophy and modern cognitive therapy have had in their own lives.[10]

Marcus and the Stoics played a large role in my life as well, in my professional studies in cognitive psychotherapy, in my avocation of ethical philosophy, and in my own spiritual journey.

I had come across bits and pieces of the writings of Seneca in my youth, but he had the most profound effect on me in my early 40s. Having gone through a doctoral program while working full-time, teaching on the side, and raising young boys with my wife, it was after encountering one of his pithy remarks in the spring of 2004 that I decided I'd work on the side as a professor no more. That decision in turn led to the chain of events that year that brought me back to Christ and His Church. The quotation was this: "*Nihil nimis est hominis occupati quam vivere*"—"There is nothing the busy man is less busied with than living." And of course by this he means the man who is *too* busy, he who has scheduled his life in such a way that he has left little time for leisure and reflection. Socrates, a hero to the Stoics, put it this way: "The unexamined life is not worth living."[11]

To make a long story short, it was when I had obtained that leisure which Seneca advised that I found myself freer to focus on my own moral purpose à la Epictetus—and before long, like Marcus Aurelius, to say of all things and events around me, "This has come from God."

---

10. Prominent among these individuals include Jules Evans, who was so moved that he traveled to the U.S. to interview Albert Ellis before his death, and has gone on to preach the Stoic gospel everywhere from lecture halls to pubs to rugby players' locker rooms. See Evans's *Philosophy for Life and Other Dangerous Situations: Ancient Philosophy for Modern Problems* (Novato, CA: New World Library, 2012).

11. I would recall later another quotation from Christ on a not dissimilar theme: "Martha, Martha, you are anxious and troubled about many things; one thing is needful. Mary has chosen the good portion, which shall not be taken away from her" (Luke 10:41). (The needful thing is the love and contemplation of God.)

The Porch and the Cross

To make that short story long, the roles of Seneca, Epictetus, and Marcus Aurelius in my own journey of faith and reason is the subject of Chapter 7, *Stoic Strivings: The Slave, the Lawyer, the Emperor, and God*, of my own memoir *From Atheism to Catholicism: How Scientists and Philosophers Led Me to Truth* (Our Sunday Visitor, 2010).[12]

But now it is time to sum up this book, to move from Aurelius's porch to the cross of Christ—to see how the wisdom of the ancient Stoics can make *us* wiser and more loving Christians *today.*

12. That chapter was also excerpted on the Stoicism Today web site on 3/21/15. http://blogs.exeter.ac.uk/stoicismtoday/?s=the+porch+and+the+cross.

Conclusion

Bringing Stoic Wisdom and Christian Love into Our World Today

No longer talk about the kind of man a good man ought to be, but be one.

~ Marcus Aurelius[1]

In truth, sublime words make not a man holy and just: but a virtuous life maketh him dear to God.

~ Thomas à Kempis[2]

Sanity, Integrity, Humanity, and Nobility

While pondering the biographical chapters I'd write for this book, I asked myself what single word I could use to describe each of our four Stoics.[3]

For Musonius Rufus my word of choice was *sanity*. He said in his 21st lecture that "thoughtlessness is very near to insanity" and few were more thought*ful* than he about more important things. I trusted that many moderns would be especially surprised by the things Musonius said about women, marriage, children, the family, and sane sexuality. His thoughts should challenge the sanity of the course that our modern world is taking on those issues.

---

1. Long, *Meditations,* 108.
2. Thomas à Kempis, *My Imitation of Christ* (Brooklyn: The Fraternity of the Precious Blood, 1954), 5.
3. You might note that these words appear in each man's "Legacies" chapter title.

For Epictetus I chose *integrity,* though the same could be said of Musonius and of Marcus. The words *freedom* or *autonomy* were also strong contenders. In a person of integrity, thought, word, and deed are as one. In Epictetus, Stoic philosophy, Stoic teaching, and Stoic behavior were as one and made flesh in his Stoic mode of living.

For Seneca my choice was *humanity*; for he was human, all too human, in weakness and in folly, but in high aspirations and benevolent sentiments and actions too. He reminds me of a story of St. Martin de Porres, a 16th-century Dominican brother and patron saint of social justice.

Martin once overheard an old friar berating a young one because the youth was wearing a fancy pair of shoes. After all, every Dominican had taken a vow of poverty. Martin pulled the old friar aside and told him that perhaps some poor sinner would decline to make a confession to a friar who seemed so much holier than he, but upon seeing a man with a taste for fashionable shoes he might feel he could understand him, and then go ahead and unburden his soul to the less daunting, more worldly, well-shod confessor.

For some of us, perhaps Seneca will be our friar with the fine, expensive shoes. Here is a man who understands how truly hard it can be to forsake the allures of the world and focus solely on virtue and God, and yet he tried throughout his life and exhorted us to do likewise. He may well proffer useful advice for healing our own far-less-than-perfect human souls.

Last, but never least, my choice for Marcus Aurelius was *nobility*; not nobility in the sense that he descended from kings and aristocrats, but in the sense that even though he descended from a king and ascended to the throne of emperor he did not think overmuch of himself, but focused all his energies on virtue, honor, and duty.

We've surveyed a sample of key lessons of these four men from the porch. They provide instruction for all men and women; and as for those of us who are Christians, they still provide valuable lessons in how we can become saner, of greater integrity, more fully human, and nobler. St. Irenaeus (130–202) wrote in his *Against Heresies* that "the glory of God is man fully alive, and the life of man is the vision of God."

These Stoics have provided many lessons, deduced from natural reason without the benefit of Christian revelation, but in many essential points consistent with Christian ethics—lessons than help us become more fully alive, better glorifying God by leading us to keep our eyes and hearts on Him. Our goal here is not to make Christians of the ancient Stoics so much as to borrow the ancient wisdom of those Stoics to help *us* become better Christians.

Let's conclude by looking at some lessons from these teachers we can carry from their porch out into our world.

Spiritual Exercises to
Perfect the Art of Living

Our four Roman Stoics pursued philosophy as a guide to the art of living, as a means to transform and improve our life through the cultivation of our God-given reason. Christians are called through Christ to a total transformation as well, a transformation calling for *faith* in addition to but not opposed to *reason*, promising the ultimate end of eternal life, as well as a transformed life here on earth. What would Jesus Christ proclaim as the ultimate guide to the Christian art of living? We do know the answer to that one:

> You shall love the Lord your God with all your heart, and with all your soul, and with all your mind. This is the great and first commandment. And a second is like it: You shall love your neighbor as yourself. On these two commandments depend all the law and the prophets. (Matthew 22:37–40)

Here is the answer that sums up the both the natural law discernible by human reason and the direct revelation of God as passed on through the prophets. We are to love and follow God first of all, and to love both others and ourselves as well. We have examined key teachings of the Stoics, and I think it is safe to say that they would be in agreement on this point. We are indeed to follow God, to act with benevolence toward the universal brotherhood of men and women, and to honor ourselves in the pursuit of virtue. Though the Stoics did not know Christ, and their Stoic conceptions were not and could not be completely compatible with the Christian faith, *the important question for Christians today is whether or not ancient*

Stoic wisdom can help us fulfill those ultimate commandments laid out so clearly by Christ.

Part III of the modern *Catechism of the Catholic Church* is entitled "Life in Christ." Its key topics include how man is made in the image of God; the nature of human happiness, of freedom, of good and evil acts, of the passions, the virtues, and sins; of our roles in society, of justice and moral law, of the Ten Commandments, and of prayer. The Stoics spoke either directly or indirectly to the subject matter of all of these issues. They too were conscious of being made in the image and likeness of God; and through their deep understanding of that human nature, they can provide us with tools to control our own passions and tendencies toward sin, to grow in hatred of vice and sin, to grow in the love of virtue and duty, and all in a spirit of gratitude toward God and a fervent desire to live according to His will.

The Stoic art of living is not acquired merely through a reading of the Stoics accompanied by an appropriate "Aha!" at their insights. Each Stoic makes it clear that *to live a life guided by philosophy requires repeated and persistent efforts.* It takes ongoing, strenuous training throughout the course of one's life in the form of *askesis,* philosophical and spiritual exercises. Look back in our chapter 2 to Rufus's Lecture 6, on the practice of philosophy, and you will get a basic glimpse at the Stoic call to physical and spiritual self-training. It is akin to the self-training recommended early on by such Christians such as St. Clement of Alexandria (150–215) and to the spiritual exercises later fully developed by St. Ignatius Loyola (1491–1556). There are many such "exercises" that can be culled from the writings of our four Stoics if one is willing to dig deep and read with a discerning eye. Fortunately, several modern authors have already done so for us.[4] I will merely provide a quick and limited sampler of Stoic spiritual exercises.

---

4. For readers who would care to dig deeper into the Stoics' practical spiritual exercises as an integral part of an art of living, I direct readers to Pierre Hadot's *Philosophy as a Way of Life,* John Sellars' *The Art of Living,* Donald Robertson's *The Philosophy of Cognitive Behavioral Therapy,* and Elen Buzare's *Stoic Spiritual Exercises.*

A Swift Sampler of
Stoic Spiritual Exercises

There are many components to proper training of the body. There are different exercises for different muscle-groups and for the acquisition of a variety of abilities and skills, from strength, to endurance, to flexibility, to the coordination and expertise required for a host of different sports or other physical endeavors. Exercises must be repeated on a regular basis, starting with what is easy and ever progressing as the body adapts. There are a great variety of spiritual exercises as well that call into play in different ways various mental powers, such as our capacities for imagination, visualization, memory, reasoning, language, reading, writing, praying, and interacting with others. As health and fitness are to the body, virtues are to the soul.[5] Virtues are perfections of our God-given powers, and we also need to exercise them so that they may grow.

At many points in their writings, quite a few of which have been captured in the summaries within this book, Musonius Rufus, Epictetus, Seneca, and Marcus Aurelius all recommend and describe a variety of practical exercises to train oneself up in the Stoic art of living; so here comes our quick sampler:

Memorization—To employ Stoic insights to control our passions, discern and seek out only what is truly good, and happily follow God, we must *internalize* fundamental principles and maxims, like Epictetus's emphasis on the need to distinguish what is within our control and what isn't, and his insistence that things don't disturb us, but only our judgments about things. There are many ways to do this, including the use of the *method of loci*, an ancient "art of memory" using visual imagery techniques that is itself a product of ancient Greco-Roman and medieval Catholic cooperation throughout the centuries. Indeed, in the words of memory historian Frances Yates, "If Simonides was the inventor of the art of memory, and 'Tulius' its teacher, Thomas Aquinas became something like its

---

5. "Virtue, inasmuch as it is a suitable disposition of the soul, is like health and beauty, which are suitable dispositions of the body." St. Thomas Aquinas, *Summa Theologica* I, Q. 55, a.2.

patron saint."[6] Yates's book provides the fascinating history of this art, and I have produced two detailed and illustrated guided tutorials applying the methods to Catholic catechesis and apologetics.[7] It can be used just as well to memorize key principles and maxims of golden wisdom from the Stoic philosophers.

Writing—Epictetus explicitly advised his students to write down key ideas as a means to help internalize and more deeply understand them. (Thankfully, Arrian took his teacher's advice—otherwise we might know very little of Epictetus!) The greatest example we have of this Stoic exercise as *self-training* is Aurelius's *Meditations*. The greatest example of written correspondence as Stoic *training for others* is in the great bounty of Seneca's *Letters*. I've tried to do my part by writing this book. In what manner might *you* use writing to grow in Stoic virtue?

Daily Rituals—Feel like just lying in bed? Recall how Marcus would cajole himself to get up to do the day's work of a man. Recall too how he would prepare himself each day to meet with "the busybody, the thankless, the overbearing, the treacherous, the envious, the unneighborly," forgiving them in advance for acting that way out of ignorance. And as for the end of the day, recall Seneca's habit of reviewing his day and examining his conscience every night before he went to sleep. Epictetus tells us that the person who has mastered philosophy will remain safe and secure, following God even while asleep. Perhaps Seneca's nightly reflection will help in that regard.

Meditation on Grand Themes—We see this exercise repeatedly in Marcus's *Meditations*. We can help contain our petty passions, disturbances, and fears when we see our lives in the context of the big picture, by picturing the goings-on of all the earth from a perspective high in the sky; by contemplating the vastness of the universe,

6. Frances A. Yates, *The Art of Memory* (Chicago: University of Chicago Press, 1974), 82.

7. *Memorize the Faith!* (*And Most Anything Else*) *Using the Methods of the Great Catholic Medieval Memory Masters* (Manchester, NH: Sophia Institute Press, 2006) and *Memorize the Reasons! Defending the Faith with the Catholic Art of Memory* (Catholic Answers Press, 2013). *Memorize the Mass!* is on the way, and perhaps even someday a *Memorize Epictetus!*

the inevitably of death, the fact that all the great people and important happenings from centuries past are no more, and that our life on earth is also ever changing and passing.

Catching First Movements—Epictetus advised us to examine our impressions, and Seneca was particularly adept at analyzing the internal psychological steps and processes that occur when we succumb to passions such as anger. He knew, as all Stoics did, that we are disturbed not by things but by the views that we take of them, because we possess the power of reason and can examine and judge all external events or impressions. Still, we share with other animals innate, reflexive, emotional responses. Hurt us physically, and thoughts of anger may rise as quickly as the physical pain. Present us with an erotic image, and physiological responses will instantly begin. We cannot prevent these "first movements," these fleeting, reflexive, "automatic thoughts," as some modern cognitive therapists call them; but we can train ourselves to examine them, and to prevent ourselves from acting on them until we've had time to bring our reasoned judgment into play.

Alphabetize!—Here I refer not so much to an explicit ancient Stoic technique as to Ellis's ABC model of emotion built upon Stoic thought (especially the fifth chapter of Epictetus's *Enchiridion*), the model I laid out in brief in this book's chapter 6. When something happens that disturbs you, remember that this is an A (activating event), which does not cause your C (disturbing emotional consequence) without the consent of your B (belief or judgment). If you D (dispute) any belief that leads you to seek or avoid something that is outside your control, you can end up with a newer, saner, calmer, more loving and more Christ-like E (emotional consequences). If you would like to develop emotional self-control, this is a Stoical exercise worth practicing every day.

Grabbing the Right Handle—Recall from chapter 43 of the *Enchiridion* that "everything has two handles, and only one of them is suitable for carrying." If your brother insults you, don't grab the handle of insult, but the handle of the fact that he is your brother. We should train ourselves to always seek to grab the right handle— the nobler, truer, more virtuous one. We might even "handle" the Stoics themselves this way: "Seneca was vain and wrote in places that men could be greater than gods. He, like the other Stoics, glorified suicide. Epictetus sure did not seem too sympathetic to the hardship of others. Aurelius was so resigned and melancholy, and he did not prevent the martyrdoms of Christians." "Why yes, but they too were your brothers. They too were made in the image of God. They carried that divine spark of the Holy Spirit within them, and despite their human faults they shared so many great truths with us that we should gladly thank our mutual Father for them."

Stoic Wisdom / Christian Love

Their rather murky concepts of God notwithstanding, the Stoics acknowledged him based on reason alone, because they had not met Christ. Nonetheless, they also deduced from God's existence our need to live lives of virtue, honor, tranquility, and self-control, and they developed very effective techniques to help us achieve this. The ancient Stoics still provide a practical technology for putting Christian ethics into daily practice. Christ told us that above all else we are to love God with all our hearts, and our neighbors as ourselves.[8] It is hard to practice love like that when our hearts and minds are so easily diverted and consumed by desires, passions, fears, and lusts for things outside of our control. The Stoics can help us learn and remember what is up to us and what is up to God alone. They can help us bear our crosses without complaint and show gratitude to God for the freedom he has given us in his likeness and image.

There is still much that good Christians can learn from these teachers on the porch.

8. Matt. 22:35–40, Mark 12:28–31, Luke 10:25–28, citing Deut. 6:4–5, Lev. 19:18.

76126635R00120

Made in the USA
Columbia, SC
30 August 2017